RECIPES FOR RESPECT

Southern
Foodways
Alliance

SOUTHERN FOODWAYS ALLIANCE
STUDIES IN CULTURE, PEOPLE, AND PLACE

The series explores key themes and tensions in food studies—including race, class, gender, power, and the environment—on a macroscale and also through the microstories of men and women who grow, prepare, and serve food. It presents a variety of voices, from scholars to journalists to writers of creative nonfiction.

SERIES EDITOR

John T. Edge

SERIES ADVISORY BOARD

Brett Anderson | *New Orleans Times-Picayune*

Elizabeth Engelhardt | University of North Carolina at Chapel Hill

Psyche Williams-Forson | University of Maryland at College Park

RECIPES FOR RESPECT

African American Meals
and Meaning

RAFIA ZAFAR

The University of Georgia Press
ATHENS

© 2019 by the University of Georgia Press
Athens, Georgia 30602
www.ugapress.org
All rights reserved
Set in 10.25/13.5 Minion Pro Regular by
Graphic Composition, Inc.

Most University of Georgia Press titles are
available from popular e-book vendors.

Printed digitally

Library of Congress Cataloging-in-Publication Data

Names: Zafar, Rafia, author.
Title: Recipes for respect : African American meals and
    meaning / Rafia Zafar.
Description: Athens, Georgia : University of Georgia
    Press, [2019] | Series: Southern Foodways Alliance
    studies in culture, people, and place
    Includes bibliographical references and index.
Identifiers: LCCN 2018042681 | ISBN 9780820353661
    (hardcover: alk. paper) | ISBN 9780820353678
    (paperback : alk. paper) | ISBN 9780820353654 (ebook)
Subjects: LCSH: African Americans—Food. | Food
    habits—United States. | African American cooking.
Classification: LCC E185.89.F66 Z34 2019 | DDC 641.59/
    296073—dc23
    LC record available at https://lccn.loc.gov/2018004213

for Bill, who cooks

Contents

RECIPES FOR RESPECT

Food as a Field of (Black) Action

Few chefs of African descent work at the pinnacle of our national haute cuisine today, yet their contributions to American kitchens and dining rooms have been definitive. Without their expertise, the nation's gastronomical heritage would be much the poorer. Bygone compendia such as *Charleston Receipts*, with its "quaint" illustrations of Geechee cooks, and Marjorie Kinnan Rawlings and *Cross Creek Cookery*'s sidelong nods to longtime cook Idella Parker once ruled American cookbook shelves. Such depictions of Black cooks, even if meant to be laudatory, simultaneously romanticized and belittled their efforts: their genius was untaught, their command of ingredients and techniques *a priori*. White employers served as the medium through which Black achievements could be made legible. Although recognition of African American culinary contributions is at long last arriving, Black cooks and hospitality entrepreneurs have been publishing recipe books and housekeeping guides since the 1820s.

I begin *Recipes for Respect* with anthropologist Mary Douglas's keen observation that "food is a field of social action"—an acknowledgment that societies share nourishment with some groups and withhold access from others.[1] Douglas allows us to see the intersection of food and authors as a way to understand the Black American imperative to access dignity, status, and civil rights. Since the earliest African American authors wrote poems, life histories, and essays, Black Americans have been writing their way to freedom and self-reliance. As evident in hospitality manuals of the nineteenth century and recent cookbooks celebrating African American contributions to dining in the United States, authors of African ancestry have clearly understood the role and value of cooking, serving, and eating in the pursuit of civil rights and achieving civilized lives. Black chefs and writers—sometimes one and the same—drew on their culinary and authorial skills to cook up a different form of sustenance. In kitchens, dining rooms, and restaurants, Black cooks and their foodways illustrated the truth of the claim that food—its preparation, its sharing, its denial—constitutes a landscape on which can be set the culture and progress of African America. To uncover the historical intersections of cookery, race, and genre that produced new literary forms, social mobility, and civil rights, *Recipes for Respect* defines several gastronomic crossroads—literary and culinary places and spaces—so that the hidden history of Africanisms in the American kitchen, as Toni Morrison might have it, becomes visible.[2]

Around 1930 the bibliophile Arturo Schomburg realized that recovering the gastronomy of the African diaspora would necessitate the navigation of a vast and irresistible subject. Could he limn the lives and works of the countless anonymous cooks—the "black and unknown bards" of America's kitchens?[3] Although Schomburg eventually set aside his project, he left behind a puzzle, a command, and a *sankofa*, a congeries of intentions I determined to pursue.[4] Unlike Schomburg's proposed volume, this book analyzes representative authors and texts, including Schomburg's own manuscript, rather than attempting an encyclopedic study. My book does not intend to diversify the bastions of fine dining, remake best cookbook lists, or recalibrate the minds of food columnists; my meditations are not meant to stand in for a detailed history of African Americans in the kitchen. Rather, *Recipes for Respect* contemplates cookbooks, hotelkeepers' guides, novels, and memoirs as revelatory venues for Black authors' deployment of foodways to elevate their social status, attain civil rights, and present a dignified professional self to the public. The efforts of these authors—some primarily cooks and others primarily writers—provide a powerful counterpoint to the prevailing narrative that consigned Black Americans to a visible yet low status in the country they provisioned, fed, and served.

In discerning the connections present throughout a century and a half of Black foodways and authorship, three overlapping strategies making up a veritable Venn diagram of African American cookbooks stand out for their repeated appearances. These shared concerns or tactics can be discerned in three areas: by genre, in the creation of a Black culinary history, and through the settings where cooking and eating intersect to catalyze movements for social justice. Cookbooks, generally viewed as straightforward instruction, can do double duty as memoirs and autobiographies, etiquette manuals, epistolary narratives, and even agricultural bulletins. Cookbooks provide more than the steps needed to arrive at edible meals. Collections of recipes represent experiments in genre that forward African American social mobility and respect. Thus, we see Edna Lewis writing elegy along with her recipes, Malinda Russell looking to slave narratives when introducing her cookbook, Robert Roberts offering up an etiquette manual along with instructions for other kinds of polishing, and Tunis Campbell choreographing dining room service. Meals perform work beyond satisfying hunger, and so George Washington Carver offers suggestions for plating a dish and composting a field while the Darden sisters teach us that there is more to African American cuisine than pork and greens.

The creation of a Black gastronomy, per se, may not have been foremost on the minds of most of the authors we will encounter, although each of these works help build up that history. The past was very much on the minds of men such as Schomburg, whose collection of books and ephemera formed the basis for the New York Public Library's vast collection of works on the African diaspora, and George Washington Carver, a scientist who cooked, and who understood the trajectory of small-scale agriculture; and women such as Edna Lewis and the Darden sisters, whose family-centered cookbooks told the tale of the Great Migration, its prequel, and its future motion. These writers may not have explicitly addressed the historical encounters of African-descended peoples with food, yet all spoke to that legacy.

That legacy of migration can legitimately be seen as southern. With few exceptions the South provides the foundation of much of what the authors in this study proposed and realized. To write of the slave narrative means to write of the South; to write of plantation recipes relies on an understanding of the region's histories; to be Black and American, in the years before immigration from the Caribbean and Africa began to rise, meant that almost certainly "one's people" were at some point southern-born. When author and chef Edna Lewis wrote in a posthumous essay "What Is Southern?" she invoked blackberry cobbler and the novelist Reynolds Price, hoppin' John and Martin Luther King Jr. as emblematic of the South.[5] For anyone who writes of African America knows that wherever Americans of African descent live or work, or write or cook, there lies the South: Robert Roberts, political activist and Massachusetts hospitality entrepreneur, was born a southerner, while hotelkeeper Tunis Campbell, until recently better known as a Georgia state senator, was once reviled as a carpetbagger from New Jersey. The South is a region, sometimes a geographic location and sometimes a cultural heritage, as culinary historian Michael Twitty well knows.[6]

If culinary history and literary form represent the first of two ways in which food works as a field of social action, Black American writing about meals enables civil rights activism. Cookery allows authors to draw attention to the linked domains of social justice, economic mobility, and food security. Without the successful implementation of the first, the others will not follow. Discussions of eating and dining provide windows into contests over equality. Anne Moody's memoir, for example, explicitly lays out the terms of these engagements, while the Darden sisters speak to the meaning of accessible meals. The conjunction of food and writing addresses social injustice, economic pathways, the role of cooking and the kitchen in the formation of American culture, and, not incidentally, how to make a delicious meal. The following seven chapters highlight aspects of "food as a field of action"; collectively they provide an alternative, gustatory history of African America.

The first chapter, "Recipes for Respect," asks how the earliest male chefs and authors negotiated their roles as Black men in a white-dominated society. Robert Roberts, Tunis Campbell, and Thomas Bullock each published guides that included recipes for meals and mixed drinks; two specifically provided both suggestions to employers and advice to African Americans seeking employment. They offered a script for elevating social status as well as their insights into white-Black relations. The second chapter, "Born a Slave, Died a Chef," continues my investigation into the rhetorical strategies of nineteenth- and early twentieth-century African American hospitality writers. Abby Fisher, Malinda Russell, and Rufus Estes illustrate another aspect of self-presentation through cookery. Born before the end of the Civil War, these authors engaged their postbellum white audiences by using slave narratives as prefaces and through elliptical references to enforced servitude; they show us how domestic servants parlayed their connections to whites into an entrepreneurial authorship. Engaging with the extant stereotype of ignorant Black cooks, the first century of African American hospitality authors expanded the cookbook genre, demonstrating how performance and self-presentation led to status-enhancing publication.

The next two chapters continue to take up the issue of genre, while asking a different set of questions. In "'There Is Probably No Subject More Important Than the Study of Food': George Washington Carver's Food Movement," we see the way mundane agricultural bulletins exhort the reader to cultivate and eat simply. The reigning picture of the lovable "peanut man" overlooks the Tuskegee professor's significance as an early proponent of sustainable agriculture and farm-to-table eating. Carver's dozens of extension pamphlets contained hundreds of recipes, from fruit leather to sauerkraut; they also included directions for maintaining a sustainable farm.

Food insecurity and contested commensality foster social change along with literary expression, whether inscribed in a memoir, a cookbook, or a combination of the two. "Commensality and Civil Rights" moves this study forward in time, with Anne Moody's midcentury recollections of meals served and food shared—or not. By the 1970s, the Darden sisters' *Spoonbread and Strawberry Wine*, along with the cult favorite *Vibration Cooking* by Vertamae Smart-Grosvenor, illustrate the ways Black women authors "signify on" southern and African American cookery. To these authors, making and remembering meals supplants history in a time of social upheavals; sometimes instructions for a meal offer a recipe for change. "Elegy or *Sankofa*? Edna Lewis's *Taste of Country Cooking* and the Question of Genre" argues that while cookbooks record memory, space, and history, compilations of recipes can also mourn a lost loved one or recall a vanished place; *sankofa*, the Akan word generally translated as "going back to move forward," orients this section. In *The Taste of Country Cooking*, specific individuals are recaptured, as is an entire community—not to embed Lewis's childhood home in amber, but to encourage readers to carry on African American culture.

In the last chapter, "The Negro Cooks Up His Past: Arturo Schomburg's Uncompleted Cookbook," I situate my project alongside an unfinished manuscript of the legendary book collector. One of the twentieth century's most important bibliophiles, Schomburg began but never completed a Black culinary compendium. The recipe titles he enumerated only sometimes revealed traces of the African continent, for it is a cuisine that draws from multiple culinary sources. Significantly, most of the dining rooms and kitchens central to its storytelling remain lost to this day. With this concluding section, I pay homage to the man and his enduring mission to archive the African diaspora in all its facets.

Advice, history, novel, memoir, sankofa, archive: When is a cookbook more than a set of instructions? How might a meal rewrite history? I hope that *Recipes for Respect* answers some of these questions of provender and prejudice, by reading fiction and foodways as a literary menu for a just society.

Recipes for Respect

Black Men's Hospitality Books

On the eve of the Civil War, the African American entrepreneur Eliza Potter put a question to her white readers. "Why, then, should not the hair-dresser write, as well as the physician and the clergyman? She will tell her story in simpler language; but it will be none the less truthful, none the less strange."[1] Her memoir, *A Hair Dresser's Experience in High Life*, scripted a tell-all of Cincinnati and Saratoga Springs society, and as would Mary Todd Lincoln's confidante Elizabeth Keckley in her best-selling *Behind the Scenes at the White House*, Potter revealed the fraught exchanges between white employer and Black entrepreneur. Decades before Potter and Keckley, however, African American men told of their experiences serving the white world. If the image of the Black female cook or domestic servant is more familiar to white Americans today, Black men also presided over white kitchens and households. So while the first two volumes containing cooking instructions were written by African American men, they are not in the strictest sense of the term cookbooks but early entries in the realm of "domestic economy" or housekeeping texts. These inaugural African American–authored manuals with recipes— Robert Roberts's *The House Servant's Directory* (1827) and Tunis Campbell's *Hotel Keepers, Head Waiters, and Housekeepers Guide* (1848), along with Tom Bullock's *The Ideal Bartender* (1917)—offered instructions for making soup, silver polish, and juleps. Along with their housekeeping lessons, these books revealed an unexpected facet of the Black back stairs that supported white American middle-class life.[2] They also disclosed an African American pathway to social mobility and civic respect.

Roberts, Campbell, and Bullock did not expose backstage scandals in the white world from the servant's vantage point, as had Potter and Keckley. They displayed instead the invisible labor, the "Black back regions," that made a certain kind of lifestyle possible for generations of European Americans.[3] Although none were slaves at the time they published their volumes, Bullock was born into slavery, and all labored as domestic employees within a nineteenth-century American economy that offered few career options for an ambitious Black person. The three men eschewed overt discussions of their Black selves in white America, and one doesn't even use first- or second-person pronouns to forge a personal connection with his readers. Yet between, before, and sometimes among the lines of their recipes, these hospitality workers provided recipes not only for meals but also for interracial social skills, business acumen, and negotiating power.

Robert Roberts published his *House Servant's Directory, or a Monitor for Private Families* in 1827, before the better-known doyennes of domestic economy, educator (and sister of Harriet Beecher Stowe) Catherine Beecher and abolitionist Lydia Maria Child, published theirs. Prior to that, Roberts had served as the butler to Massachusetts governor Christopher Gore. James and Lois Horton, historians of antebellum Black Boston, identified Roberts as "a community leader, serving as delegate to the Second National Convention of Free People of Color in the 1830s"; they also described him as a Garrisonian, attesting to his forthright stance on abolition.[4] As a politically aware Black man, Roberts described the Colonization Society—the putative philanthropic organization intended to send Americans of African descent back to a "home" few had any memories of or connections with—as "a clamorous, abusive, and peace disturbing combination."[5] Such a stance presents us with contradictions: on the one hand, Roberts appeared to preach a career doctrine of individual submissiveness; on the other, this former butler railed against those whites who would try to remove native-born Americans to a strange land, as did peers such as abolitionist Samuel Cornish.[6] As Graham Hodges has observed, in mid-nineteenth-century Massachusetts, whose Supreme Judicial Court abolished slavery in 1783, embedded patterns of deference between working and bourgeois classes would be difficult to avoid, especially for one born a slave in the eighteenth century. Servility would not be the only mode in which working free Blacks associated with white employers, as Hodges points out: "Roberts's insights into the personality of the head servant created a black persona capable of remaining calm and professional under very trying circumstances. . . . [We need to recognize] black men whose work mandated external deference but who conducted themselves with dignity and skill."[7] Roberts's guide includes 105 recipes for everything from "a most delicious salad sauce" (recipe 36) and "a cheap and wholesome beer" (recipe 99) to directions "to pre-vent the breath from smelling, after liquor" (recipe 90) and for compounding "Italian polish to give furniture a brilliant luster" (recipe 6). Most significant for an understanding of nineteenth-century America are Roberts's sub rosa instructions on surviving as a free Black in a white-dominated environment.

Roberts's handbook gives his readers explicit and practical guidance on "SERVANTS' WORK...THE ART OF WAITERS...FRIENDLY ADVICE TO COOKS...AND COMPLETE INSTRUCTIONS ON HOW TO BURN LEHIGH COAL" (i) at the same time as he speaks to the delicate subject of interracial etiquette. Addressing his readers in the familiar second person, Roberts demonstrates a personal stake in the business of educating servants. In his introduction, he addresses himself "to my young friends Joseph and David" (ix). Taking an avuncular tone, the former butler speaks to young col-leagues as an older, more experienced traveler in the white world of "private families" and gubernatorial households. Roberts shapes his remarks on the subject of unfair treatment with reference to biblical precedent and his experi-ence as a Black man in white America. A sincere Christian, Roberts pointedly addresses those who work for those "Private Families" to whom his work is partly addressed by casting his advice within religious parable:

> my young friends, you may perhaps find a master or a mistress who may act un-kindly and unjustly toward you, as Laban did to Jacob his servant and son-in-law; but if you do your duty honestly and faithfully, depend on it that you will be more happy in your integrity than your employers can be in their injustice; for it is much better to be the oppressed than to stand in the place of the oppressor. (xi)

In this story from Genesis, Laban—cast here as the unjust employer who bears a familial connection to his servant—and Jacob, hardworking yet unappre-ciated, translate readily into an analog of the strained connections between white American bosses, or masters, and Black Americans who, however de-graded their status, bear a family-type relation to those for whom they work. When the place of employment is a home, the metaphor of family, for whites and Blacks, served and servants, becomes hard to avoid. By referring to this tale without naming the biblical book, Roberts presumes a knowledge of the Christian Bible on behalf of his literate, almost certainly Protestant, white and Black readers. Roberts and others of his African American peers invoked scripture to draw a legible parallel between the ancient Israelites and Black Americans in slavery—a comparison that would not be lost on white readers of New England stock.[8] The butler-author thus reaches two audiences: Black workers can take pride in their own integrity, whereas the addressed white employers can recognize an implicit rebuke or a pat on the back.

The word "credit," repeated throughout the text, exposes the impossibility of a genuine family relation between the employed and the employers; the way Roberts uses this noun underscores the fragility of servant-employer relations in the early nineteenth century. "Credit" appears on a number of pages, often denoting "a source of honor or distinction"—as in the saying familiar to Black and white Americans alike, "a credit to his race." Time and again Roberts insists that to perform a task in a particular way is to ensure that approbation will follow: "Every man that lives in this capacity [as a house servant] should have a sufficient quantity of clothes to appear always neat and respectable; both for his own credit, and for the credit of the family he serves" (16); "[by following these instructions] you will find the coat folded in a manner that will gain you credit from any gentleman" (32); "you should make it your whole study to be kind and obliging to all around you, then you are sure to gain credit and esteem from every one" (70). This notion of credit, and its related attributes of "having a reputation for sound character or quality . . . [and] influence based on the good opinion or confidence of others," underlies much of Roberts's advice.[9] To peruse the lengthy full title of *The House Servant's Directory* is to understand that the author means to provide more than "FULL INSTRUCTIONS FOR CLEANING PLATE, BRASS, STEEL, GLASS, MAHOGANY"; he intends also to offer "OBSERVATIONS ON SERVANTS' BEHAVIOR TO THEIR EMPLOYERS . . . WITH FRIENDLY ADVICE TO COOKS." To "observe" does not simply mean to watch casually, as Roberts makes clear in the *Directory*; the verb also carries the sense of watching with close attention, prior to offering analysis. When he warns that "your character is your whole fortune through life; therefore you must watch over it incessantly" (xii), Roberts refers to the ability to be consistently employed and to the hypersurveillance of Black workers.

Thus we see the quandary of nineteenth-century freeborn Americans of African descent: to secure independent livelihoods, they had to adhere to prevailing patterns of master-servant hierarchy, interactions made much more difficult by the history of slavery in the American colonies, whether north or south. Within their own communities, African American men and women could and did speak out, as the annals of the Colored Conventions and Black newspapers attest.[10] Robert Roberts was among those literate Black professionals who protested racial injustice in the years before and after the Civil

War. Perhaps he might be considered only "Somewhat More Independent," as most northern "whites tried to make certain that freedmen took the menial jobs suited to a subservient caste.... Free black shopkeepers and artisans faced obstacles they would not have encountered as slave agents of white masters."[11] Perhaps personal knowledge of the many obstacles to Black success led Roberts to agitate against threats to the free Black community, not long after he advised, in the *Directory*, toleration of an employer's unfair practices. His how-to book apprises us of the tightrope between fighting for citizenship rights and the necessity of continuous employment.

Twenty years later, Tunis G. Campbell published a volume similar to Roberts's *Directory, The Hotel Keepers, Head Waiters, and Housekeepers' Guide*.[12] While relatively little is known about Roberts, Campbell's record as a Black carpetbagger in Georgia earned him a biography.[13] Both men's politics were in part formed by their experiences in hospitality: Roberts worked as a butler at the same time he participated in abolitionist activism; Campbell, following his success as hotel manager and hostelry guide author, took his talents for organization and efficiency to the Reconstruction South. In *The Sufferings of the Rev. T. G. Campbell*, the forcibly retired Black politician recounts little of his early career as a hotelkeeper. At age twenty, he describes his early desire to fight racial injustice: "In the year 1832, I formed an anti-colonization society, and then pledged myself never to leave this country, until every slave was free on American soil—unless I went to learn something, or to get help to secure their liberation."[14] A self-described "anti-slavery lecturer," Campbell chronicles his career as a Methodist minister and some of his missions to the notorious Five Points section in Lower Manhattan. Nowhere does he comment on his life as a hotelkeeper's assistant or his earlier publication.

Campbell may have seen his *Guide* as a way to monetize his skills as a butler and director of other waiters. Like Roberts's *House Servant's Directory*, Campbell's *Guide* offers suggestions on the negotiation of employer-servant and white-Black relations. His attitudes emerge between the lines, much as Roberts's ideas about class relations are revealed in his advice to his two young friends. Speaking to the white owners of hotels and inns, Campbell offers counsel on more than the right way to run a dining room: "It is necessary to make the interests of the servants and the proprietor one. And both parties must feel their identity. Thus a mutual good feeling becomes established; the interest of one becomes inseparable from the other; and the result is confidence and mutual dependence" (7–8).[15] In a smooth-running society, as in a smoothly run hotel, all sides must understand the need to work with—not just for—others. Laborers and employers need to see that their rights and claims, if not their desires and lifestyles, converge. To Campbell, a minister and a political activist, the interdependence of servant and served, Black and white, is obvious; every action on the religious, political, and business level supports or degrades this relationship.

Campbell's observations on interclass and interracial relations remain germane: "A kind word or look is never thrown away upon a servant. This should always be borne in mind by those who have servants under their care or in their employ. . . . I would therefore recommend such uniform kindness as will ensure the good will, with the necessary firmness to command the respect of a servant, as the proper course" (93). Proud of his expertise in running a tight ship, Campbell provides "authenticating documents" from a number of whites as compliments meant to underscore the author's credibility; they also echoed the letters attached to many narratives of former slaves. When his former employer writes that Campbell is "unusually intelligent, dignified, attentive, and obliging," he validates Campbell's assertions that the "good will" of the servant cannot be purchased by wages alone. Wisely Campbell advances his argument in terms attractive to an employer: pay workers good wages, and they won't steal (8).

Writing a guidebook presented two opportunities for a Black author of the time: he could of course receive additional financial compensation for his work in hospitality, but the act of serving whites presented the chance to acquire the role of author, if not expert on taste and culture. Through the written elaboration of physical work, Campbell entered into contemporary enactments of taste and culture. If, as Simon Gikandi has shown, Blacks of the eighteenth and nineteenth centuries were believed unclean and incapable of refinement, working as a manager of wait staff and hotelkeeping was one way to achieve the label of "cultured" by an unexpected or circuitous route.[16] That Campbell ran a "high class" dining room in the cosmopolitan center of the United States upends this idea of Black inferiority. Campbell's elaborately diagrammed and performed drills, about which I will say more shortly, provide us with a paradox of slavery and taste: here is a Black nineteenth-century hospitality entrepreneur demonstrating the proper way to run a white establishment. In other words, Campbell and his colleagues perform a tactic, playing a game whose terms are set by others but at which one can win nonetheless.[17] The servers' performances elaborated by Campbell showcased the taste and refinement supposedly inaccessible to Blacks.

For Campbell's success derived partly from his ability to leverage American anxieties about a literal and figurative lack of "taste" into bankable skills.[18] Exactly how a proper dinner ought to be served, when the covers for a serving dish must be removed and how far back, how many feet exactly each waiter must stand behind the chairs of the clients: such status concerns were dispelled by Campbell's reputation—the manager of a New York City hotel dining room—and his drill sergeant–like instructions, which could be used with the reader's own employees. Waiters, according to him, "should be instructed to hold themselves erect, and upon the squad drill they should be taught a regular step, the same as a military company. All should wear very light shoes or slippers, to prevent noise in walking, as no noise should be made, if possible, but the men should glide about, with a quiet, easy step" (94). The smallest aspect of serving was dictated by a man keen to set himself up as an arbiter of taste, a position desired for both financial and political reasons.[19]

While Campbell's drill describes neither a dance nor a parade, its dictated movements refer to a history of diasporic African performances stretching from the plantation South through the mid-Atlantic and into New England.[20] Although born free in Middleton, New Jersey, in 1812, Campbell grew up in a world shaped by and still entangled with slavery: a mere two years before, the state census had listed more than ten thousand slaves.[21] Although by the start of the Civil War New Jersey had seen a precipitous drop in the number of enslaved workers, individuals of African descent—even those freeborn such as Campbell—remained subject to racism and repressive legislation. Northern Black communities, like their southern counterparts, contained members with histories of enslavement or African-born relatives. Campbell's Black peers and neighbors offered continuity with a diasporic community. These intergenerational connections shaped Campbell's particular approach to hospitality.

Singled out for particular praise was "the novelty" of the serving style Campbell perfected, known in restaurant parlance as "drills." Campbell's cadre of waiters carried out their duties professionally via regimented motions. His drills, described and graphed in minute detail in the *Guide*, offered a unique take on an established practice, which he brought to a distinctively high level.[22] When we consider the movements and attire specified by Campbell, we can see such dining room rituals harking back to northern Black

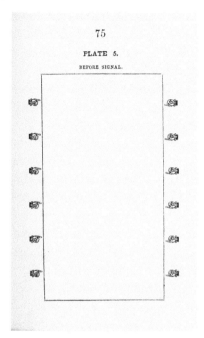

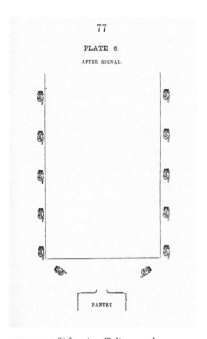

FIGURE 1.1 "Before signal" diagram indicates the placement of waiters before the meal is served. From Tunis Gulic Campbell's *Hotel Keepers, Head Waiters, and Housekeepers' Guide*, 1848. Courtesy of Michigan State Libraries.

FIGURE 1.2 "After signal" diagram shows movement of waiters from dining room to behind the scenes. From Tunis Gulic Campbell's *Hotel Keepers, Head Waiters, and Housekeepers' Guide*, 1848. Courtesy of Michigan State Libraries.

public ceremonies such as Pinkster, General (or Negro) Training, and Election Day parades that mirrored "roughly equivalent processional . . . traditions of certain African regions."[23] Campbell's drills, precisely imagined and described, drew on diasporic processions even as they followed extant notions of dining service.[24] By having his staff move around tables in ways that echoed diasporic processions, Campbell creolized, if not Africanized, Eurocentric styles of service.[25]

Diagrams detailing how and where waiters were to move illustrate the infusion of diasporic performance styles. Campbell's illustrations, I believe, offer a palimpsest of African culture via the movement and physical locations of the Black waiters. Here and elsewhere in the *Guide*, Campbell illustrates the direction servers should face, from opposite sides of the dining table (figure 1.1), and then, at the ringing of a bell, how they should march in parallel lines to the pantry to retrieve the soup (figure 1.2). Although they do not move in the counterclockwise procession noted by many scholars of slave culture, other aspects of the drill (e.g., "when they return it must be in the same order as they go out") suggest a ritual or a parade that acknowledges both the service history of European footmen and butlers and the stylized movements of free Blacks in North American festival pageantry. In ghostly form, the drill references the circular motions of West African performance styles.

Campbell's career in hotel hospitality can be called a "counter-poetics," to use Simon Gikandi's term.[26] Although his serving and dining elaborations were aimed at white Americans conscious of their "lack of refinement," he also presented, via the synchronized, semicircular movements of his drill, Mary Douglas's "food as a field of action." These performative remnants of an Afro-diasporic North laid the ground for the organizing tactics he later displayed as vice president of the Georgia Republican Party and state senator. Although his detractors would later fault him for allegedly lining his own pockets, they grudgingly acknowledged his legions of loyal constituents. Having successfully directed a hotel and its restaurant while taking care to avoid waste and to treat his staff respectfully, Campbell's skills would be well deployed during the hurly-burly of Reconstruction politics.[27]

Born in Louisville, Kentucky, around 1872, Thomas Bullock Jr., author of *The Ideal Bartender*, remains the shadowiest of these three authors. His mother had almost certainly been a slave; his father, a furniture drayman, was a former Union soldier who apparently adopted his wife's surname. In his twenties Bullock worked as a bellboy. Within a few years he was employed as a bartender, first in Louisville, then on a railroad club car; for many years, railway car work was the Black male path to the middle class. After his parents separated, Bullock cared for his mother, at one time maintaining a household that included his brother and sister-in-law and their child. Around the beginning of the twentieth century, Bullock settled in Saint Louis, perhaps after spending time there while on the road. He married and had a child, but the union did not last; within a few years of his book's publication, Bullock seemed to disappear from the Saint Louis directories. Prohibition foreclosed the job category of bartender to the wealthy, so Bullock may have moved elsewhere in search of employment.[28]

Bullock's talents behind the bar were highly regarded, first in his position as bartender for the Pendennis Club of Louisville and afterward at the elite

Saint Louis Country Club. Bullock's prodigious skills as a "mixologist" led him to a moment on the national stage. George Herbert Walker, a wealthy and influential white businessman (and the grandfather and great-grandfather of George H. W. and George W. Bush, respectively), memorialized Bullock in much the same way other white men had introduced many a slave narrative. In the preface to *The Ideal Bartender*, Walker lauds Bullock's skills via an "authenticating document" that tells the story of the crossed paths of Theodore Roosevelt and the Saint Louis bartender. Perhaps Walker, who wrote that "it is a genuine privilege to be permitted to testify to his qualifications" (5), was the individual who suggested that Bullock include the editorial from the *St. Louis Post-Dispatch* that pointed to the supposedly temperate presidential candidate's only having drunk part of one of Bullock's famed mint juleps. The editor scoffed at Roosevelt's equivocation, writing that for a "red-blooded man, and a true Colonel at that" not to drain to the dregs a julep composed by Mr. Bullock "strain[s] credulity too far."[29] Bullock never says what he thought of his ancillary part in a presidential candidate's public relations debacle; with the briefest of comment, the editorial is reproduced as "a testimonial" to Bullock's genuinely intoxicating touch. And like the best barkeeps, Bullock spread no tales of conversations overheard or advice given. The dozens of drink recipes (including a few free of alcohol for the rising temperance-minded set) appear without reference to his firsthand knowledge of the socially connected.

As could be expected from one born in horse-racing country, Bullock includes not one but two julep recipes. One is for "Mint Julep—Kentucky Style" (which calls for a silver mug, a lump of sugar, water, ice, "Old Bourbon Whiskey," and mint), a second for "Overall Julep—St. Louis Style" (which strays far from the accepted julep formula by omitting the bourbon and using rye whiskey, "Gordon Gin," grenadine, lemon, lime, and "Imported Club Soda").[30] None of the recipes even fleetingly refer to the author's life; his personal history remains shielded behind the welcoming yet reserved demeanor presented in the volume's photographic frontispiece (figure 1.3). To regard Bullock's tuxedo-clad image, and his face creased by the barest of smiles, calls to mind once more Graham Russell Hodges's remark about the all-too-frequent necessity for a Black man to perform service work under trying conditions, which may have nothing to do with the physical state of his kitchen and everything to do with his clientele. If there were times he was confronted with belligerent racism or

FIGURE 1.3 Tom Bullock, from the frontispiece of *The Ideal Bartender*. Courtesy of Michigan State Libraries.

drunken ignorance, we get no hint from either text or photograph. An exemplary professional, Bullock presents his time-tested and renowned mixtures with no glimpse of the man within.

As Earl Lewis has noted, skilled African American men such as Bullock, Roberts, and Campbell had to balance—if not mute—personal desires for civil rights with the concomitant wish to elevate their social status.[31] Despite social disadvantages, African Americans turned skills learned in bond or free domestic service into entrepreneurial and political careers. Writing up the results, tangible and otherwise, of lives in service, Black Americans could transform their manual labor into a less physically taxing livelihood. By obliquely propounding ideas of racial independence, individual achievement, and economic self-sufficiency, Black men such as Campbell, Roberts, and Bullock variously negotiated interracial relations. Embedding recipes within explanatory passages allowed them to speak to such ideas as personal credit or self-satisfaction. Black and white readers gained more than instruction.[32] Published cookbooks, guides for wealthy homeowners, and advice to hotelkeepers allow us to peer into the fraught world of social and professional obligations. To read such Black-authored books as simple templates for household expertise would be to miss their accompanying recipes for respect.

Born a Slave, Died a Chef

Slave Narratives and the Beginnings
of Culinary Memoir

The figure of the enslaved Black cook was already a stereotype by the mid-nineteenth century; historians note that real-life Black female household chefs were relatively rare in antebellum America, yet Harriet Beecher Stowe's best-selling *Uncle Tom's Cabin* (1852), with its detailed depictions of two Black women cooks, fixed that persona in the nation's consciousness.[1] At the same time that Stowe cemented the female slave's place in the kitchen, autobiographies of the formerly enslaved were also best sellers; they appeared in the form of as-told-to pamphlets, nonfiction essays, or entire volumes. If a slave narrative—often authenticated by interpolated letters from admirers or former owners, reproductions of marriage licenses, or free papers—functions as an authenticating document to a collection of recipes, how does the life of one formerly enslaved function as a prologue for the instructions that follow?

When a cookbook's preface or introduction relates the author's personal history of bondage, the reader might consume—and I use the word deliberately and analogously to Kyla Tompkins—the recipes that follow differently than those that do not appear with such authentication.[2] To be precise, although full-time Black cooks may have been present in a minority of slaveholder homes, the presence of those cooks in the national imaginary was outsized and would continue to grow in the twentieth century.[3] As enshrined in the popular imagination, the true artists of the kitchen were Black women; therefore, Black-authored cookbooks would carry an authority earned during the antebellum period. Therefore, when slave narratives or their echoes preface and haunt early Black recipe collections, they function powerfully as authenticating documents, like the white-authored testimonials that prefaced the memoirs of bondage: the chef's personal experience of slavery confirms the expertise of the author.[4]

Confounding the stereotype of the Black woman cook, the earliest fictional depiction of an African American in the kitchen may well be the male slave Caesar in James Fenimore Cooper's second novel, *The Spy* (1821), in which George Washington figures as a minor character. Cooper's Caesar could in fact have been based on two Black chefs enslaved by U.S. founding fathers—chefs who, like the earliest authors of cookbooks and hospitality guides, were men. Hercules, Washington's self-emancipated cook, has only recently become part of our national narrative; in his lifetime he was rarely mentioned in contemporary letters and memoirs.[5] Similarly, James Hemings's presence as a historical actor was known to intimates and correspondents of the second president, even if he cooked for Thomas Jefferson largely during his French sojourn as secretary of state, not in the White House.[6] Acknowledged during their lifetimes as gifted men, they left no memoirs or cookbooks for posterity.[7] Midway through the first century of American nationhood, that absence began to change.

After the Civil War, cookbooks written by African American southerners began to appear. These publications aimed to instruct in culinary matters more than did the earlier volumes more accurately described as hospitality handbooks. Malinda Russell's *A Domestic Cook Book: Containing a Careful Selection of Useful Receipts for the Kitchen* (1866), *What Mrs. [Abby] Fisher Knows about Old Southern Cooking* (1881), and *Good Things to Eat* by Rufus Estes (1911) were entirely about prepared foods, offering recipes for a wide range of meal items, from infant pap to roasts to éclairs. Their volumes document a nascent Black middle class of hospitality entrepreneurs.[8] Russell and Estes further distinguished their works by their unique deployment of what has been called the indigenous American literary genre, the slave narrative.[9] Fisher, although she does not explicitly identify herself as a former slave, gestures briefly and nearly unnoticeably to an early life spent in a slave society.[10] These manuals inaugurated the canon of Black-authored cookbooks; they also heralded a form, the life story with recipes. Later twentieth-century innovations owe as much to William Wells Brown and Harriet Wilson as they do to Catherine Beecher and Amelia Simmons, said to be the author of the first American cookbook.

Russell, Fisher, and Estes each share their talents along with their knowledge of the peculiar institution. Their books address the enslavement experiences of their families and communities. As we have already seen, the earliest African American cookery authors provided invisible labor, enabling a more leisurely lifestyle for white middle- and upper-class employers.[11] Free citizens at the time they published their volumes, Fisher, Estes, and Russell were nonetheless shaped by the peculiar institution. Although all three worked for pay by the time they became authors, their cookbooks paradoxically yoked current expertise with a past marked by bondage. Their publications were extensions of their careers, illuminating U.S. culinary history and African American business acumen and social mobility.

Combining a cookbook with a slave narrative offers the implied audience a curious set of choices: Does one read to learn how to bake gingersnaps, or does one read to learn of injustice overcome and the bright future ahead of a dark past? Can one book do both? Russell and Estes, who explicitly invoke slavery, address a white postbellum audience that would deem the continued reception of slave narratives beside the point—the Civil War had freed the slaves. In terms of the emotional landscape of the postbellum years, some literary scholars have asserted that the later memoirs of former slaves demonstrate a desire for reunion, an attempt to bring together warring sides for the nation to heal and progress.[12] In their cookbooks, a former slave and the grandchild of a slave present unusual venues for reconciliation: the kitchen and the dining room. By offering recipes and instructions that conjure up the antebellum United States without focusing specifically on southern cuisine, Russell and Estes provide a gastronomic détente. They self-authenticate their productions, briefly acknowledging who they are and how they became equipped to write their cookbooks.[13]

Malinda Russell's *Cook Book* advertises itself on the title page as the production of "an experienced cook." Russell's first modern editor, culinary historian Jan Longone, identified the pamphlet as the earliest known cookbook by an African American.[14] Rightly pointing to Russell's historical significance, Longone refers us to the author's self-identification as freeborn: "My mother being born after the emancipation of my grandmother, her children are by law free" (3). Russell had never been enslaved, although her grandmother had suffered under that infamy. Despite the legal status of children on the freeborn side of *partus sequitur ventrem*, Blacks were still subject to white opprobrium, violence, and crime, as readers of Russell's "A Short History of the Author" discover. The passage of the Thirteenth, Fourteenth, and Fifteenth Amendments did not prevent slavery's legacy of displacement and danger from shaping the lives of African American southerners. The slave narrative, abbreviated and twice removed, would serve Russell well, establishing her racial bona fides as chef and cookbook author.

Following the tradition of countless slave narrators, including Venture Smith in the eighteenth century and Harriet Jacobs at the onset of the Civil War, Russell begins her cookbook with the words "I was born." Adding that her birth took place in Washington County, Tennessee, and that she was raised in Green County in the same state, Russell notes that she is "a member of one of the first families set free by Mr. Noddie, of Virginia" (3), a prestige-claiming identification with a "First Family of Virginia" that many of her readers would have understood. When it refers to Black families, such an invocation exudes irony; it is a rhetorical if subconscious move, supported by Russell's later use of the word "faithful," itself an adjective applied to the author by white employers, inviting nostalgic thoughts of loyal Black servants. In keeping with the travails recorded by many enslaved narrators, Russell relates various incidents during her flight out of the South in which she is tricked, including by a member of her own party traveling to Liberia (first she was robbed—"a considerable sum . . . was taken from me [in 1864] by a guerilla party, who threatened my life") and subsequently "attacked several times" (4). These misfortunes, coupled with the early death of her husband and the birth of a disabled child, mark her as a woman beleaguered by personal setbacks and continued racial discrimination and violence. Nevertheless, Russell's self-confidence, which we also see in Abby Fisher, persists. She publishes her cookbook to raise money to support herself and her child, believing it "will sell well where I have cooked" and satisfy those who follow her instructions (4). The penultimate sentence of "My History" ends with the hope that the monies earned will "enable me to return *home*" (4, my emphasis). That may strike us as a puzzling remark for someone who referred to her northern home as "the Garden of the West" (4).[15] But such sentiments are not entirely surprising, given her stated intention to recover her property and reunite with friends and family—and that to this day African American families long established in the North continue to refer to southern states as home.[16]

Russell's choice of publisher and northern home places her in the company of numerous ex-slave narrators. Like others, she follows the North Star to Michigan, a Union state known for its stops on the Underground Railroad and by some referred to as a "garden," a reference to its Edenic symbolism. She was undoubtedly aware that Detroit was a frequent point of departure for slaves headed for Canada, for Michigan was thought of as a state hospitable to Blacks. If we look at the bottom of her book's cover page, we discover that her printer was one T. O. Ward, editor and publisher of the *True Northerner*—a newspaper located in Paw Paw, across the state from that gateway to freedom. Founded in 1855, the *True Northerner* was a Republican paper forthright about its Union sympathies, referring to the "blighting curse" of slavery.[17] The politics of the newspaper, coupled with front-page advertisements announcing the printer's availability for "job work," made it a desirable option for the African American author. Russell trusted her entry into the world of cookery to a firm she believed would be fair to a person of her race. That only one copy is known to have survived may speak to the small press's limited promotion of the work and the actual number of copies printed.[18]

Russell looked to a work already seen as a classic for her model, advising her readers that she cooked on the plan of Mary Randolph's *The Virginia House-wife* (5). Novice authors and their advertisers would assert that an author or a book was like one already familiar and beloved.[19] If most of Russell's recipes could appear in any English-language cookbook published in North America, "Sweet Potato Baked Pudding" and "Sweet Potato Slice Pie" (22–23) would more likely appear in cookbooks south of the Mason-Dixon Line. "How to Cook and Dress Ocher [okra]" (36) similarly points to southern, African diasporic cuisine. More specifically, Russell acknowledges her apprenticeship at the hands of "colored" Virginia cook Fanny Steward, whose life and identity remain in shadow (ix). We cannot know whether Russell's recipes were developed by her, culled from an earlier printed text, or orally transmitted by Steward. Furthermore, if Fanny Steward shared memories of life in slavery, we do not learn of them. Russell's preface and the historical record afford few clues, and those that remain tantalize.

Some years following the Civil War, after Russell became an author, the southern-born Abby Fisher began a new life in California. She too sought to parlay her expertise as a baker and cook into entrepreneurial success and the higher-status role of author. Fisher's preface reveals the balancing act performed by Black Americans dependent on white patronage for their social mobility:

> The publication of a book on my knowledge and experience of Southern Cooking, Pickle and Jelly Making, has been frequently asked of me by my lady friends and patrons in Francisco and Oakland, and also by ladies of Sacramento during the State Fair in 1879. Not being able to read or write myself, and my husband also having been without the advantages of an education—upon whom would devolve the writing of the book at my dictation—caused me to doubt whether I would be able to present a work that would give perfect satisfaction. But, after due

consideration, I concluded to bring forward a book of my knowledge—based on an experience of upwards of thirty-five years—in the art of cooking.[20]

In 1881 Fisher became the fourth African American to publish a book containing recipes, and the second Black American woman to publish a cookbook. Unlike Russell, Fisher does not in her book explicitly take up matters of slavery, sexual oppression, and racial discrimination. Her instructions to readers allude to a lifestyle defined by entertaining; no mention is made of servitude. Some Black authors writing during the latter part of the nineteenth century may have sensed that, with the Civil War over and the Gilded Age begun, white American concern with the struggles of the formerly enslaved had reached a low point—although, as we have seen with Russell (and later will see with Estes), that belief was not universal. Perhaps because it was published in California, a jurisdiction admitted to the Union as a free state, *What Mrs. Fisher Knows about Old Southern Cooking* does not refer to slavery or indenture.[21] Its "complete instructor" gave readers seeking the right way to pickle or to form a croquette only the barest glimpse of the author's private life. Yet while obliquely delineated, Fisher's experiences as a Black woman shaped her place in American cookery.

After the Civil War ended, earning a living took precedence over literacy, which Fisher tacitly acknowledges in her preface and "apology." Still, her educational disability didn't lead her to abandon the project: "Not being able to read or write myself . . . caused me to doubt whether I would be able to present a book." The cook's forthright personality and self-possession, buttressed by her years as a sought-after caterer, convinced her to pursue the status of author. Hers was not a false modesty guided by rhetorical convention, for following her introduction Fisher appends a list of the well-off San Francisco patrons on whose support she could rely. Her customers valued her culinary skills, and the chef correctly saw her talents as bankable. Her confidence leads her to attest that anyone can duplicate her successes: when Fisher allows that a "child" can follow her instructions, we readers understand that an inept white middle-class reader can follow them as well.

The antebellum attitude that legally or informally denied literacy and citizenship to those of African descent also kept thousands from knowledge of their families and their own beginnings. As the Black abolitionist Frederick Douglass once observed, plantation slaves knew "as little of their age as horses know of theirs."[22] As anticipated, little factual material has been uncovered about Abby Fisher's early life; what has been learned about her may be about as much as she herself knew. Initially Fisher was not even known to be an African American, as her book did not so identify her. This could have stemmed from a desire to be viewed as a chef-caterer, rather than a member of an oppressed group seeking patronage. Publishing her book under the auspices of a regional woman's publishing cooperative could also simply indicate that because her sponsors knew her, she did not need to include a biography or résumé. Much of what we know today about Fisher came about through the efforts of culinary historian Karen Hess, who tells us that the author was born circa 1832 in South Carolina, was married to an Alexander C. Fisher (born in Alabama), and was listed in a San Francisco city directory of 1880 as a manufacturer of pickles.[23] Fisher's own words reveal a bit more.

Brief references to Fisher's previous life in the South, and possibly to her place within a plantation slavery system, appear within the context of three recipes: a recipe for hoe cake, another for a health tonic, and a third for infant food (recipes 9, 102, and 160). The first recipe, "Plantation Corn Bread or Hoe Cake," does not necessarily guarantee a Black or southern-born author. Cookbook compilers of the day regularly borrowed recipes from other texts, and whites and Blacks alike consumed corn bread. Her recipe records the preparation of "Hoe Cake" but does not address the slave practice of baking a meal on the flat side of a heated hoe while in the fields; she merely directs her readers to bake the mixture on a hot griddle (11). The second recipe could suggest more of an insider's knowledge; the instructions for blackberry syrup include this comment with the daily dosage: "This is an old Southern plantation remedy among colored people" (50). Still, the recipe could have been borrowed or written from other than firsthand knowledge.

The third reference to the past, in the very last recipe of Fisher's book, reveals the most about the author and elliptically gestures toward her southern, Black origins. In fewer than two dozen words, readers hear again the self-possession evident in the book's opening paragraph. Closing her recipe for "Pap for Infant Diet," Fisher concludes, "I have given birth to eleven children and raised them all," surely a resounding endorsement of this baby food. Any prior reticence about her past—a hesitation that led to the nearly complete lack of references to her origins—is subordinated to an irrepressible pride in her success as a Black mother. Reading her words more than a hundred years later, one finds the significance of her racialized maternal identity striking. Fisher and her contemporaries knew the odds of any woman of that time having birthed and raised eleven children; even among well-to-do whites, the infant mortality rate made early motherhood an uneasy waiting game. As a Black woman or a former slave, Abby Fisher takes this achievement into the realm of the extraordinary: she birthed all of those children and reared them as well. Fisher's quiet affirmation can be seen as an open secret, a hidden-in-plain-view boast.

Fisher's children, reared by a proud and loving mother, complicate assumptions that Fisher had simply or only been a slave. When her maternal history is viewed in the context of her assigned racial category (in the U.S. census of 1880 she is counted as a "mulatto"), it seems likely that Fisher had been a favored slave, rather than a near-anonymous kitchen worker. Self-identified as the offspring of a French father, possibly light-skinned, Fisher can boast of her maternity because her status was out of the ordinary. Fair-skinned African American children of planters could receive somewhat better treatment than their peers, even if they could also be the targets of jealous mistresses. The luckiest sometimes gained the sanctity of their own nuclear families or manumission at adulthood.[24] The personal history that once distinguished her as an enslaved parent may also have been one she was quite willing to efface, once she became an author. Including no framing narrative to satisfy speculation, Fisher left her readers only a few clues.

Coming at the close of her 160th recipe, Fisher's seemingly offhand remark about motherhood identifies the unusual nature of her endeavors. Her achievements, buried among the culinary tasks that she details, nearly go unnoticed. Like many of the era's striving Black women, committed to a "politics of respectability" bent on expunging centuries of Black female stereotypes, Fisher might have meant to shield her private life.[25] To be a Black woman in the pre-Emancipation era was to be thought no more enterprising than livestock, to be sexually assaulted with impunity, and to give birth without security. Few facts of Abby Fisher's life before she arrived in California thus emerged within her text. But even in a free state, slavery figured as a palimpsest in American cookery.

The history of American bondage was included forthrightly in Rufus Estes's self-published *Good Things to Eat, as Suggested by Rufus: A Collection of Practical Recipes for Preparing Meats, Game, Fowl, Fish, Puddings, Pastries, Etc.* (1911). Although it was common to secure a private printer in the nineteenth century, Estes's choice of a private publisher may also point to the difficulty that Black authors had securing the sponsorship of a regional or national publisher. Like Fisher and Russell before him, Estes used his culinary talents to rise up and away from slavery-shadowed beginnings. As a Pullman chef, he was part of the growing Black middle class. Like his peer Booker T. Washington, Estes was born Black, in bondage, and without citizenship.[26] If not as spectacular as Washington's, Estes's rise was remarkable nonetheless.

Rufus Estes wanted to be known as an accomplished chef *and* a former slave. To be both underscored the professional heights to which he had climbed. *Good Things to Eat* begins with a foreword then proceeds to a "Sketch of My Life." In the opening paragraphs Estes offers the vernacular wisdom that parents frequently overlook the faults of their children, be those offspring flesh and blood or paper, but he avers that he "has honestly striven to avoid this common prejudice . . . [and] frankly admits [that his book] is not without its faults." Nevertheless, *Good Things to Eat* "will serve in a humble way some useful purpose" (5). As Fisher had done three decades earlier, Estes offers the expected declaration of modesty while simultaneously asserting the worthiness of his project. All the recipes, he claims, were written down during moments "snatched" from his daily duties. The book's very appearance stemmed from the urgings of the powerful patrons whom Estes served, "some of whom have now become his stanchest [*sic*] friends," (5) who told him again and again to write a cookbook. Gratefully Estes dedicates the volume to those white friends and patrons who encouraged him (6), enabling him to add the occupation of "author" to his résumé.

Although whites figured prominently in his earliest years, they did not offer implicit imprimatur to Estes, as had the cooperative that published Abby Fisher's volume or the antislavery newspaper that printed Malinda Russell's. Unlike the explicit encomia appended by Robert Roberts and Tunis Campbell, Estes included no letters attesting to his skills. Instead, the Pullman chef self-authenticated his text with his own chronicle of involuntary servitude. Beginning, as do most published slave narratives, with the incantation "I was born," Estes's "Sketch of My Life" outlines the childhood and young adult years of his former self. This former slave would later list his address as the Appomattox Club, Chicago's "prestigious black republican social club."[27] Born into the world as the supposed possession of D. J. Estes in Murray County, Tennessee, Estes was his mother's ninth and last child. The coming of the Civil War in his home county inspired nearly all male slaves of sufficient age to join the Union forces. One of the children left behind, Estes learned "to carry water from the spring . . . drive the cows . . . mind the calves . . . gather chips, etc." (7). When

Estes was about ten, he and his mother moved to Nashville, where he attended school for a single term; although education for Blacks was now legal, putting bread on the table was paramount. Generically and historically, Estes's life story connects him with antebellum autobiographers such as Frederick Douglass, who similarly described his lack of formal schooling and first wages.

Before divulging even a single recipe developed over a praiseworthy career, Estes shares his biography; only then does he offer up "good things to eat." The arc of Estes's life seems to predict his culinary career: after his move to Nashville, he took a job toting meals to agricultural workers, earning a quarter from each man per month, although "all this, of course, went to my mother" (7). From sixteen to twenty-one years of age he worked at a restaurant, and not long after that he headed north to Chicago. In 1883 he was hired by the Pullman service and was subsequently "selected to handle all special parties," beginning a public career as a chef. His customers included Presidents Cleveland and Harrison, musicians Ignacy Paderewski and Adelina Patti, and Princess Eulalie of Spain. In the mid-1880s, Estes sailed to Japan in private service. By the end of the century he had settled into his career as chef, first on a private railway car and later "for the subsidiary companies of the United States Steel Corporation in Chicago" (7).

His life story told, the cookbook follows. Going forward, his authorial persona rarely intrudes, although occasionally Estes adds an aside, as when he indicates "my own preference" in steak is for one not "burned to a cinder, but slightly scorched over a very hot fire" ("Broiling Steak" 28). "Hints to Kitchen Maids" (8) shares tips with less experienced workers, suggesting, for example, how much breakfast to serve to "a person employed indoors" (8). Unlike Robert Roberts a century earlier, who advised inexperienced domestics, Estes's remarks are less avuncular and more professional. Estes does not set himself up as a kitchen autocrat as he makes clear when closing his advice column, writing that "the above [ideas] are merely suggestions that have been of material assistance to me" (8). Nonetheless, his "suggestions" assert a well-managed pride in his professional success.

As a cookbook author Estes includes no "delicacies that would awaken the jaded appetite of the gourmet" (5), offering clear, straightforward instructions for "Mushrooms in Cream" and "Fried Hamburg Steak, with Russian Sauce." Despite his comment about world-weary palates, Estes points out that many of the meals his readers can now create could serve for either "the home table or banquet board" (6). Rarefied items such as "Crystallized Cowslips . . . a prized

English confection" (103) can be reproduced with his assistance. More typical are instructions for familiar fare, as with the previously mentioned steak, "Scalloped Shrimps" (20), "Glazed Carrots with Peas" (68), "Whole Wheat Bread" (84), or "Fresh Raspberry Pie" (88). Despite fifty recipes for "Beef, Veal, and Pork" (there are also chapters on poultry and game), entrées are overshadowed by dozens of recipes for "Pies and Pastries," "Cakes, Crullers, and Eclairs," "Candies," and "Ice Cream and Sherbets." A final exegesis on sugary treats titled "Desserts" completes the assortment. Is Estes's sweet tooth a personal inclination or subconscious compensation for Black America's bitter travails? Rather than descend into the psychoanalytic or biographical fallacy, I will paraphrase Freud and attest that sometimes an éclair is just an éclair: as other scholars have noted, nineteenth-century home cooks needed more instruction in baking, preserving, and candy making than they did for fixing meat and potatoes. Estes's presentation of a slave narrative before he shares his recipes for roasts, pies, and confections invites his audience to recognize the connection between his minor celebrity and the skills earned during an early life impoverished by bondage and lack of formal education.

Rufus L. Estes, Malinda Russell, and Abby Fisher, like their predecessors in hotel- and housekeeping, forthrightly if briefly contemplated the relationship between Black creator and white consumer. Along with cooking and baking skills, they developed entrepreneurial talents and elevated their social status. Whether to a significant or nearly unnoticeable degree, each leveraged knowledge of servitude as a confirmation of culinary ability. In the course of their transformation from worker to author, Russell, Fisher, and Estes foreshadow a hybrid seen in many cookbooks of the twentieth century and beyond: the memoir with recipes. By prefacing their selection of recipes and instructions with a narrative that recalls the author's personal experience of slavery or that of her family, or by elliptically referring to a life of bondage, they begin the multigeneric cookbook. If the cookery volumes of Mary Randolph and her kin attest to the delectable expertise of their authors, those of Estes, Fisher, and Russell go further. By connecting the Black American past of involuntary cookery and household management to their hard-earned successes, the earliest African American cookbook writers bent toward their own interests and stereotypes of the Black cook and racialized nostalgia. Some may have been born as slaves, but they died as chefs.

"There Is Probably No Subject More Important Than the Study of Food"

George Washington Carver's
Food Movement

From his early experiences as a former slave searching for education in his native Missouri, to his unprecedented achievement of a master's of science in botany from Iowa State University, to his long academic tenure at the Tuskegee Institute in the heart of segregated Alabama, George Washington Carver was determined to access the knowledge and career that most white Americans would have denied him. He knew as a child that education would be an important part of his future: "When just a mere tot . . . my very soul thirsted for an education. . . . I wanted to know every strange stone, flowers, insect, bird, or beast. No one could tell me [what I wanted to know]."[1] As so many Americans know now, the little boy whose curiosity knew no limits grew up to be what was then nearly unheard of: a Black man with an advanced degree. His elite education could have led him in a number of directions, including a permanent faculty position at Iowa State, but Carver believed that God and his race directed him to the South generally and Tuskegee Institute in Macon County, Alabama, specifically. His zeal for knowledge of the natural world and determination to improve the lives of the everyday Black farmer never flagged.

Carver was a botanist whose domain extended beyond the discovery and categorization of plant species. In his autobiography, he recalls his boyhood affection for wild and tended plants, calling them his "pets" and noting that neighbors called him "the plant doctor" when he was so young he "could hardly read."[2] Historian Linda McMurray described him as both "scientist and symbol" and addressed the potent mythography that still swirls around the man. More recently, environmental historian Mark Hersey has explored Carver's legacy, celebrating him as a conservationist whose race and Christian spirituality led to his erasure from studies of early twentieth-century naturalists.[3] To call Carver a civil rights activist who focused on food, in the way of Anne Moody of Mississippi, also is incomplete.[4] His career led to an increased respect for Black intellect and scientific prowess; his life constituted its own, if indirect, debunking of white superiority. The plant scientist was publicly reticent on the subject of civil rights, much in the way of his employer Booker T. Washington, founder and first leader of Tuskegee. Yet Carver promoted racial harmony through his Christian affiliations, his willingness to accept speaking engagements at white institutions, and his work with white businessmen and politicians. Rather than view Carver from a specific and single perspective, I would like to add another dimension to the portrait of Black professor and scientist: early proponent of what we now call sustainable agriculture and farm-to-table eating. Whereas today's locavores are often gastronomic elites seeking the latest iterations of haute cuisine, Carver urged rural agriculturalists to rely on their own gardens for ingredients rather than store-bought purchases. The Iowa-trained botanist would become one of the most ardent proponents of the self-reliant ideology developed by the charismatic Washington. As Jennifer Jensen Wallach has shown, Washington believed firmly in the role of cookery and dining to elevate African Americans, "continually advocat[ing] for a food system managed by and for Black people. He believed that food practices were an important means of preparing the Black population for first-class citizenship."[5] Carver seemed predestined for the Tuskegee faculty.

Carver's childhood was unusual for one born into slavery: after losing both parents as a small child, he was raised by his former owners, the Carvers. In some ways he was treated almost like a foster son, albeit with the limitations defined by Black parentage. While his brother Jim, also raised by Moses and Susan Carver, was "tall, robust, and husky" and later worked as their "hired labor" until shortly before his death from smallpox, George was from an early age "frail and sickly" and possibly tubercular.[6] Because of his health problems the younger Carver spent much of his time outdoors exploring small creatures and plants, rather than performing tasks such as logging or haying ("I literally lived in the woods").[7] Susan Carver assigned the child household tasks, including cooking and crocheting. These skills would later prove crucial when he moved from place to place in search of an advanced education. Following his initial move from the Carver home, he again became a foster child of sorts, this time to a Black couple: Mariah and Andrew Watkins. Mariah Watkins's culinary skills and familiarity with the medicinal uses of herbs furthered

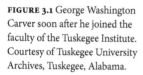

FIGURE 3.1 George Washington Carver soon after he joined the faculty of the Tuskegee Institute. Courtesy of Tuskegee University Archives, Tuskegee, Alabama.

Carver's interest in plants and how they might be used for human consumption and medical applications. His desire to extend his schooling once more led him from home. Carver's acquired skills allowed him to cook for a living, and he later recalled that in his teens he "was cooking for a wealthy family in Ft. Scott Kansas for my board, clothes and school privileges"; subsequently, Carver worked "as first cook in a large hotel" in Winterset, Iowa (see figure 3.2).[8] After being refused admission on racial grounds to a school in Kansas, Carver supported himself with his domestic talents; to earn room and board at Simpson College and then at Iowa State, he ran laundry services. These experiences, especially his stints as cook, account for the household hints, recipes, and cooking suggestions he would incorporate in future publications. Like Robert Roberts, Carver used his skills in service to augment a later career; in his case, Tuskegee Institute would sponsor his "cookbooks."

Carver arrived in Alabama in 1896, after receiving his master's degree in scientific agriculture from Iowa State. He would spend the rest of his academic life at the Tuskegee Institute. Due to the reign of Washington, its charismatic and devoted founder, Tuskegee was then the most renowned historically Black college in the world. During the exchange of letters with Washington that led

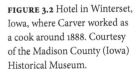

FIGURE 3.2 Hotel in Winterset, Iowa, where Carver worked as a cook around 1888. Courtesy of the Madison County (Iowa) Historical Museum.

to Carver's hire, the scientist confessed, "I expect . . . to go to my people and I have been looking for some time at Tuskegee with favor."[9] Like that of Tuskegee's founder, Carver's life and career would become inextricably linked with the institution.[10] His eccentricities would also become part of campus lore— like his daily donning of a fresh flower boutonniere, climbing the fire escape to his apartment in the women's dormitory building, and knitting his own socks. Often refusing gifts of attire, Carver would wear and repair his own clothes until they were close to rags: biographer Rackham Holt stated that Carver wore the same suit to the 1937 unveiling of his commemorative bust at Tuskegee as he did for his graduation from Iowa State in 1896.[11]

Washington hired Carver to run the agriculture department. The botanist spent some of his early career managing the campus poultry farm, attempting to start an apiary, and launching a trial silkworm colony. Unfortunately, Carver lacked the aptitude to balance academic administration and animal husbandry: the high mortality rate of the school's chickens, to name just one failure, drew criticism from Washington and eventually led to Carver's dismissal from poultry duties. As interested in research as teaching, Carver did not aspire to be a dean or campus administrator, whatever Washington's plans for him had been. Carver's professional relationship with Washington can fairly be described as turbulent, in fact. Yet when Washington died before reaching his sixtieth birthday, the botanist rued the many times the two had exchanged words.[12]

Despite their differences, Carver and Washington admired each other's abilities and would have admitted that the other's celebrity positively impacted his own life's work. That did not stop Carver from threatening on more than one occasion to take his professorship elsewhere. Carver's fame frequently rests on the many experiments he performed that led to new and surprising uses for common agricultural products such as peanuts and sweet potatoes. Overlooked in the celebration of his entrepreneurial science is the impetus for his move to the Deep South: his desire to become a race man by aiding the farmers who labored with little to show for their efforts but debt. In a nation now roiled by debates over genetically modified organisms (i.e., GMO food crops), Carver's "old-fashioned" methods of composting, installing kitchen gardens, and conscious eating seem simultaneously quaint and prescient. He should be lauded as an avatar of responsible land stewardship and healthy meals.

At Tuskegee, industrial education ruled the day. Even taking into account Carver's predilection for research, teaching was expected to be a major component of his duties. The classroom eventually did take a back seat to his research and public presentations; Carver's disinterest in administrative details possibly spilled over into a dislike for the minutiae of grade books. Nonetheless, he displayed an Emersonian belief in the natural world as an extension of the classroom. His 1910 bulletin *Nature Study and Gardening for Rural Schools* lays out his experiential approach to education, which at Tuskegee included having his classes compete with one another collecting specimens. Students were amazed by their professor's ability to identify seemingly any plant brought to his attention. Other pedagogical successes included outreach efforts such as appearances at state fairs and farm visits, conducted at a time when the agricultural extension movement was just getting under way.[13] Remarkably, due to Washington's canny and determined efforts, Tuskegee was granted agricultural extension school status in 1897 despite the fact that it was not a land grant college. As part of Tuskegee's extension mission and beginning in 1898, Carver wrote and published numerous bulletins which were circulated gratis to the small farmer, whether Black or white; initial print runs were of two to five thousand copies.[14] In addition to offering instructions on growing cotton successfully on sandy soils—a lesson to be expected from a historically Black school in the Cotton Belt—Carver's pamphlets laid out directions for raising, preserving, and preparing fruits and vegetables. He worked diligently to improve the lives of Black farmers.[15] Carver's suggestions included how to use organic methods when cultivating fruit and vegetables and the multiple reasons for doing so. He also instructed readers in methods of cooking, preserv-

CLASS IN COOKING

FIGURE 3.3 A page from Booker T. Washington's *Working with the Hands: Being a Sequel to Up from Slavery Covering the Author's Experiences in Industrial Training at Tuskegee* shows students cooking. Photograph by Frances Benjamin Johnston. Courtesy of the Schomburg Center for Research in Black Culture, Photographs & Prints Division.

ing, and eating homegrown produce. In the late nineteenth and early twentieth centuries, Carver knew that growing local crops was fiscally prudent and environmentally sound. Tuskegee bulletins advocated sensible and affordable farming methods and published literally hundreds of recipes.

Unlike his contemporary Rufus L. Estes, the Black Pullman chef, Carver was not writing a cookbook for those who craved dining-car dainties.[16] Instead, Carver's bulletins for the average farming family were aimed at people unlikely to be served in a railway car.[17] Carver's ingredients and instructions appear in the modern style that begins with a listing of ingredients and then proceeds to the how-to. He deemed some foods so versatile that he offered multiple bulletins on the same crop (or perhaps demand called for repeated publications). The prosaic cowpea received four bulletin treatments, with Carver proposing everyday dishes such as "creamed peas," "Alabama baked peas," and "hopping john." A true booster, Carver said that cowpeas should take their place in gastronomic lore along with more highly regarded legumes such as the "White, Soup, Navy or Boston Bean" (4).[18] He claimed each American region had its signature legume.

Three Delicious Meals Every Day for the Farmer (Bulletin no. 32, 1916) offers an attractive dining experience for those of modest means often believed to be uninterested in such meals. Long before today's hobby gardeners began putting up crocks of sauerkraut from their own cabbages and composting their kitchen errors, Carver opens with a gentle scolding: "We are wasteful. . . . Ignorance in the kitchen is one of the worst curses that ever affected humanity" (3). In keeping with earlier vegetarian advocates such as William Alcott and Alexander Graham, Carver warns against the "bad preparation" of meals and the perils of "bad combinations" (3) of food. The botanist lauds the healthy and "medicinal value" of homegrown fruits and vegetables "when wisely prepared" (4), and he includes a week's worth of menus featuring such dishes as sliced tomatoes and onions, green corn fritters, and homemade sausage. Some recipes use pork fat or bacon, but vegetarian dishes such as tomato soup and nut sandwiches also are embraced. The meals are advertised as "every day" and "delicious" in large measure because the cook's ingredients are either obtained from the farm's own kitchen garden or perhaps by local bartering. Carver knew that locally grown foods prepared in the farmer's home would be healthier and less expensive than store-bought goods, which provided a fraction of the nutritional value at a much higher cost. Carver's desire to bring self-sufficiency *and* tasty meals to the struggling agricultural worker was every bit as revolutionary and creative as his famed experiments that led to peanut-hull–based wallboard. He knew that planting cotton on every available scrap of land increased the likelihood that a Black farmer would remain in poverty. While Carver understood commercial fertilizer to be an occasional necessity, he emphasized that the proper use of forest and farm compost could work just as well as chemical treatments to reinvigorate worn-out soils.[19] Such advocacy contrasted with contemporary preferences for modern methods and business opportunities over cost-saving measures for the small farmer. Carver's biographer Linda McMurray has written that "small-scale, simple technology, practiced by a black sharecropper, was overshadowed by the lure of mass production technology."[20] Similarly, Carver's promotion of kitchen gardens and home-cooked meals has been overlooked to this day.

The full extent of Carver's food and nutritional activism may remain unknown. Few records from the earliest years of his career exist, as a 1947 fire in the Carver Library destroyed much of the material extant before 1920. His own writings offer little detail about his culinary experiences. (The 1943 biography by Rackham Holt is based on numerous conversations with Carver,

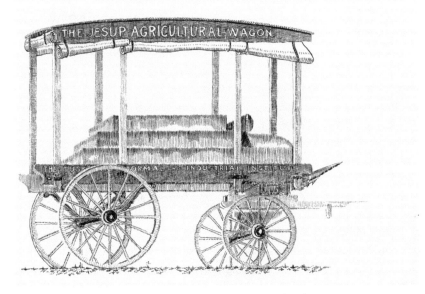

FIGURE 3.4 Carver's sketch of his Jesup Wagon reveals the scientist's early training and facility in art. Courtesy of Tuskegee University Archives, Tuskegee, Alabama.

but many anecdotes rely on decades-old memories.) How can we fully assess Carver's impact on food beyond what is available in the archive and Tuskegee publications? How could Carver reach the farmer unable to access the information printed in the bulletins because he or she could not read? One clue may lie in the Jesup Wagon, named by Booker T. Washington for the financier who funded Carver. While he did not personally staff the Jesup Wagon (that role would be assumed by his former student Thomas Campbell). Carver did accompany the Jesup's prototype into the community, as Campbell, the U.S. Food and Drug Administration's first Black extension agent, recalled: "in those earl[iest] years it was Dr. Carver's custom, in addition to his regular work, to put a few tools and demonstration exhibits in a buggy and set out . . . to visit rural areas near Tuskegee. . . . He would give practical demonstrations, both varied and seasonal."[21] Because such mobile schools aimed to educate the entire farm family, they presented complementary demonstrations on the proper use of agricultural tools and the healthful preparation of food.[22] Rather than wait for farmers to visit the extension station, Carver went to them: in current terminology, his was a "pop-up" agricultural school; as cooking lessons were sometimes included, we might even call it an early food truck. Low literacy rates kept many farmers from utilizing the wealth of information contained in the pamphlets, so Carver's classroom on wheels included advice on healthful eating as well as cultivation techniques. The Jesup Wagon and its predecessor were aimed at all farmers, educated or not, whether plowing the land or preserving its bounty. Carver's bulletins for Tuskegee provided a script for self-reliance and dignified living accompanied by recipes within the reach of modest but aspiring households; vehicular classrooms served a similar purpose.

Carver's extracurricular work on behalf of the small farmer, like the pithy advice of his bulletins, has been overlooked. A pragmatist who did not reject the judicial use of commercial fertilizer, he also knew that the poorest farmer risked financial disaster by spending scarce cash on chemical products promising to increase agricultural yields. Instead, following the injunction of Washington's parable to "cast down one's bucket where one stands," Carver urged his neighbors to be self-reliant, depending on what they could produce on their own. To pull up decaying organic matter rather than fresh water, as in the story Washington recounted—was wise advice on several levels. Nonetheless, Carver's pragmatic outlook led him to work with business and political interests that lauded him as a "cookstove chemist." If whites saw Carver's inventions as creations that could be monetized or deployed as advertisements for regional "progress," Carver evidently felt such proclamations would eventually redound to the benefit of his people.[23] These goals of helping the small farmer by advocating self-sufficiency and supporting agribusiness appear to be at odds, but Carver must have hoped that his renown in the business and political spheres would pay dividends in the future to rural Blacks. From Washington's era until the present day, many critics have said that the Tuskegee doctrine of self-sufficiency countermanded much of the rhetoric of modernization. Carver's noted peer W. E. B. Du Bois urged higher education and professionalization as key to gaining civil rights and self-respect, arguing for uplifting the peasant class and any with the ability to rise. Washington's rejection of elite schooling may have stemmed from a concern that the Black peasantry would become an unskilled, if educated, class of consumers lacking entrepreneurial capacity. The wizard of Tuskegee worried that African Americans relying on store-bought food rather than their own productions could ensnare themselves in a cycle of dependence. Yet even Washington conceded that Black America would eventually have both skilled farmers and language instruction.[24] Carver's Tuskegee bulletins promoted both food security and nourishment beyond eating.

Instead of purchasing canned goods, meat, and dairy from local grocers, Carver declared that the farmer should practice self-reliance, a theme he sounded regularly through the three-plus decades the Tuskegee pamphlets appeared. In his preface to *The Canning and Preserving of Fruits and Vegetables in the Home*, Washington "endorse[s] all that Professor Carver has said . . . and [I] urge colored farmers throughout Macon County to put into practice what he has suggested" (2). Carver begins this bulletin by noting that "fully two-thirds of our fruit and tons of vegetables go to waste," and he tempts his readers with "delicious" dried peach or strawberry leather, to name but one of his simple and electricity-free methods of preserving food (3, 6). His directions enabled the small farmer to put up foods for eating throughout the year. Carver continued his encomia to culinary freedom in bulletins such as *How to Grow the Tomato*, in which he gives recipes for fresh tomato dishes ("No. 4, Tomatoes Broiled") and also for preserves ("No. 16, Tomatoes as Olives or Vermont Olives" and "No. 100, Tomato Sauce, [Commercial Style]"). The bulletins give instructions for preparing pantry staples such as flour and mock "cocoanut" and are as useful today as they were then, when many had yet to benefit from rural electrification projects.

Carver did not limit his advice to domesticated fruits and vegetables, pointing his readers to the bounty around them free for the taking. In *43 Ways to Save the Wild Plum Crop*, Carver laments the foods available for foraging that go unused annually: "I feel safe in saying that in Macon County [Alabama] alone there are many hundreds of bushels of plums that go to waste every year" (Bulletin no. 34, April 1917, 3). The wild plum provided delicious material for pies and soups, Carver pointed out, suggesting that "no fruit makes more delicious jams, jellies, preserves, marmalades, etc." (4). He urged his readers to try a number of appealing recipes, including some for mock olives, catsup, and "Plum Lozenges (Very Fine)." (Along with his editorials, "very fine" or "delicious" were often appended as suffixes to recipe titles, much in the way that Irma Rombauer of *Joy of Cooking* fame would add "Cockaigne" to identify dishes she particularly liked.) Carver even occasionally suggests ways to plate a dish, as in his injunction to "decorate [the finished result] artistically with nut kernels" (11).

Wild plums would be an obvious delicacy to anyone walking through a southeastern forest, as would other large wild fruits, such as persimmons.

Carver, however, did not stop with the most obvious edibles. In his World War II–era bulletin "Nature's Garden for Victory and Peace" (no. 43, 1942)— the reference to victory gardens is unmistakable—Carver gives the publication an epigraph, a four-stanza poem by popular poet Martha Martin, "The Weed's Philosophy."[25] In this verse an anthropomorphized weed laments its outcast status in a world that would destroy it: "If a purpose divine is in all things decreed / Then there must be some benefit from me a—weed!" Carver's quotation emphasizes the beneficial nature of uncultivated plants. That becomes clear when he then cites the publication of a 1942 article in the *Alabama Journal* titled "Don't Worry If War Causes Green Vegetable Shortage, Weeds Are Good to Eat," referring to the subsequent letters that come to his attention asking if this claim has merit (5). Carver goes on to discuss a number of such "weeds," from dandelions to purslane and lamb's-quarters, illustrating the essay with several of his botanical drawings.[26] Donning his chef's toque, the botanist gives general instructions for serving and cooking various greens; the most formal recipe describes a dandelion salad, augmented with chopped radishes, onion, and parsley, and garnished with pickled beets and hard-boiled eggs (6). He closes with the hope that everyone will make these wild delicacies part of an everyday diet for as long as these foods are in season (18). Those reared on the work of back-to-nature guru Euell Gibbons, whose foraging handbooks shot to fame in the 1960s, should know that he had a precursor on the faculty of Tuskegee.

Foraging for wild foods was part of Carver's legacy. Contemporary students of foodways and counterculture eating habits may be familiar with this American tradition, even if they do not trace one of its adherents to Tuskegee. Carver's suggestions to turn toward wild plants to add healthy and thrifty meals to the rural Black American's diet was in fact preceded by an even earlier wartime publication, "Twelve Ways to Meet the New Economic Conditions in the South" (1917), and revisited ten years later in "How to Make and Save Money on the Farm" (Bulletin no. 39). The question-and-answer format provides guidance for farmers struggling with the depredations of the boll weevil, the tyranny of cotton monoculture, the subsequent depletion of the soil, and the inability of most farmers, renters, or owners to get ahead financially. Presented as twelve queries that small farmers were likely to pose followed by workable solutions obtainable through ingenuity and planning, the pamphlet includes tips that go beyond utilitarian instructions.

Beginning with suggestions for avoiding the worst of the boll weevil's destructive impact, Carver describes how the cash-strapped farmer could still fertilize soil depleted by cotton cropping. He notes that the demonstration plot at Tuskegee had achieved success through compost application and crop rotation, and he encourages keeping a small number of domesticated animals and planting a garden and fruit trees. The farmer "can realize more money [from crops such as corn, peanuts, and sweet potatoes] than from cotton"; even if a "paying market cannot be had for the raw product, they should be fed to stock, and turned into milk, meat, butter, eggs, lard, etc." ("Twelve," 6). Not just landowners but sharecroppers and renters should pursue these suggestions, as "it will leave more money in your pockets, aside from the great value of forming correct habits of living" ("Twelve," 7). The later bulletin includes numerous recipes culled from other Tuskegee bulletins, including directions for drying and preserving pumpkins, preservation techniques first outlined in a 1915 publication, *When, What and How to Can and Preserve Fruits and Vegetables in the Home* (Bulletin no. 27). Before both world wars, Carver asserted the ability of the small farmer not simply to survive but to thrive.

Important to our understanding of Carver is his belief in an existence where work is complemented with beauty, that science and art go hand in hand. Recognizing that hard labor deserves more than material reward, he suggests the cultivation of "a pretty door-yard with flowers." A well-landscaped home may raise the value of a property, but he notes as well that sometimes "all we need is a bunch of beautiful flowers from loving hands" ("Twelve," 7).[27] Carver may have been a professor of agricultural science, but he was also an artist, anticipating Alice Walker's recognition of how her mother's beautiful flower beds eased the struggle of their family: "Because of her creativity with her flowers, even my memories of poverty are seen through a screen of blooms—sunflowers, petunias, roses, dahlias, forsythia, spirea, delphiniums, verbena."[28] Even tomatoes were good for more than nutrition: "There are so many sizes, colors and varieties that, for garnishings, fancy soups, and especially fine decorative table effects, they are almost indispensable" ("How to Grow the Tomato," 3). In Carver the scientist and the artist coexisted, and he inspired a similar propagation of talents in others, whatever their status in life.

The life and career of George Washington Carver, known to generations of Americans as the peanut man, has been overdue for reassessment. His calls to the impoverished Black farmer to eschew commodity foods and to dine well from the products of his own and his neighbors' plots resonate in today's lifestyle pages. His appeals for healthy homegrown food preceded public health alarms calling for greater access to whole, non–genetically modified, unprocessed foods for all Americans.[29] Will Allen, recognized with a MacArthur Fellowship for his work in urban farming, may be better known today as the Black man who brought fruits and vegetables to the impoverished African American, but the noted urban farm activist gives Carver his due as inspiration and predecessor, even including Carver's illustration of the Jesup Wagon in his memoir: "I was not the first African American farmer and teacher to make trips through the South to teach people how to farm. The educator and agriculturalist George Washington Carver has long served as an inspiration to me. . . . My workshops at Growing Power were in the spirit of Carver's own [lessons]."[30] Perhaps we should not be surprised that Rodale Press's first issue of *Organic Gardening* appeared in 1943, the last year of George Washington Carver's life. Carver's baton was ready to be passed, even if decades would follow before his advocacy would be recognized.

4

Civil Rights and Commensality
Meaning and Meals in Ernest Gaines, Anne Moody, and Alice Walker

In Walt Whitman's acknowledgment of a multiracial America, the poet averred that "every atom belonging to me as good belongs to you," going so far as to claim he was one with "the hounded slave." Years before the segregation of public spaces was legally prohibited, the poet valorized a communal table including the "heavy-lipp'd slave," a place where the African American is seated among fellow humans, with "the wicked just the same as the righteous."[1] Whitman's fictive common table welcoming downtrodden, criminal, and above-reproach diners alike might have reflected the poet's effusive expansiveness, but his vision of an inclusive America was, African American poet Langston Hughes well knew, utopian. In his own verse Hughes, born ten years after Whitman's death, signifies on Whitman's catalog of multicultural Americans with an implied question: If these former slaves and descendants of former bondmen and women are equal before the law, why are they still compelled to eat apart?

> *I am the darker brother.*
> *They send me to eat in the kitchen*
> *When company comes,*
> *But I laugh,*
> *And eat well,*
> *And grow strong.*[2]

In writing of being denied a place at America's table, Hughes acknowledges the role of commensality—the practice of eating together, or more properly, commensality denied, in maintaining racial boundaries. To see the intertwined roles of eating and American civil liberties, and the way food is deployed in the making of civil rights, is to view the inner workings of the founding myth of

"*E pluribus unum.*" The conjunction of civil rights, cookery, and commensality allows us to understand how the act of dining mirrors inclusion or inequity.

Writers in the years following the apogee of the civil rights and Black Power movements expressed concerns, hopes, and determination through stories of meals denied and food shared. Three books from that period—Anne Moody's *Coming of Age in Mississippi* (1968), Alice Walker's *Meridian* (1976), and Ernest Gaines's *A Gathering of Old Men* (1983)—repeatedly designate food sharing as a field of action for civil rights. The American South of the 1960s became identified with meals denied, a place where interracial dining seemed impossible. Although recipes do not appear in the pages of these books, each text offers implicit instructions on achieving a world in which a child of sharecroppers not only has enough to eat but may also sit down to a meal with the children of the landowners.

Two of these books portray civil rights activists ensnared in the violence that occurs when groups transgress boundaries at mealtimes. Anne Moody and Alice Walker were both born in the rural South. As children they worked in the fields; as teenagers they attended historically Black colleges; as young activists they joined the civil rights movement. Moody enlisted with the Congress of Racial Equality (CORE), the Student Nonviolent Coordinating Committee (SNCC), and the National Association for the Advancement of Colored People (NAACP) in direct actions such as sit-ins; Walker registered voters and taught literacy skills and Black history.[3] Each was acutely aware of the ways in which white supremacists tried to retain power. Denying the vote to African Americans was one tactic in a seemingly endless campaign to maintain white superiority; denying access to decent jobs and homes was another crucial strategy. The refusal to grant the simple act of commensality—"to give a ruthless twist to . . . hospitality"—would be the most pointedly symbolic of racist efforts to humiliate African Americans.[4] In their books, Moody and Walker, who had been on the front lines, drew from their own experiences and those of their peers.

In *Coming of Age in Mississippi*, Anne Moody explicitly addresses the fraught nature of interracial commensality and the inequality that prevents such togetherness.[5] Known for her courageous stands against white southern terrorism, a stony-faced Moody was captured along with fellow activists in an iconic 1963 photograph, frequently reproduced in U.S. history textbooks, withstanding the abuse of white racists at a luncheon counter sit-in in Jackson, Mississippi. Moody's memoir, which takes her from an impoverished childhood

FIGURE 4.1 In this May 28, 1963, file photograph, a group of whites poured sugar, ketchup, and mustard over the heads of Tougaloo College student demonstrators at a Woolworth's lunch counter sit-in in downtown Jackson, Mississippi. (Photographed by Fred Blackwell.)

through years of struggle to her college graduation, makes clear the powerful role that food plays in shaping a person's experience of self and worth. Each of the book's four sections—"Childhood," "High School," "College," and "The Movement"—contains at least one pivotal scene about food or commensality.

The events of "Childhood" reveal the origins of Moody's activism. Her earliest years were shaped by hunger; as a toddler, she was left all day with her infant sister in the care of her eight-year-old uncle while her sharecropper parents worked long hours in the fields. The baby had "a bottle of sweetening water" (5) to satisfy her hunger and pacify her fretfulness; the older children received little more than a plate of beans. As Moody writes, when her mother returns in the evenings and tells her eldest daughter stories about the white landowners, the child doesn't dwell on the furnishings of that brightly lit house but on the "tea cakes" that she learns are baking in the kitchen.[6] Following their parents' separation, the children and their mother live with relatives, who grumble that they barely have enough food for themselves. Moody's mother finds two jobs that will afford them their own little run-down house, with leftovers from a white employer's kitchen "all we had to eat" (13). Shortly thereafter she lands a job at a "Negro café." The family's fortunes improve, but Moody's early years are scarred by stomach-churning poverty, if lightened by memories of her family's gleaning skills. My mother "had a special way of stealing the corn that made it look just like the crows had taken it" (14), while Uncle Ed caught small fish that they'd "scrape and cook . . . right on the bank of the creek. On those days we didn't have to eat the hard cold pone Mama left for us" (21).

As a child Moody learned

> that white folks ate different from us. They had all different kinds of food with meat and all. We always just had beans and bread. One Saturday the white lady [for whom Mrs. Moody then worked] let Mama bring us to her house. We sat on the back porch until the white family finished eating. Then Mama brought us in the house and sat us at the table and we finished up the food. It was the first time I had seen the inside of a white family's kitchen. That kitchen was pretty, all white and shiny. Mama had cooked that food we were eating, too. "If Mama only had a kitchen like this of her own," I thought, "she would cook better food for us." (29)[7]

The reader sees clearly that the culinary shame of financially strapped Black mothers and wives was not a relic of the past.[8]

Soon after her epiphany about the differences between white and Black kitchens, Moody begins earning her first quarters. A nearby white woman sells clabber milk (buttermilk) to local Blacks for a very low price; when the nine-year-old Moody goes with a quarter to buy a gallon, the woman also asks her to sweep her walks. The girl complies and goes home not only with the milk but also the change she brought to buy it. It's a heady feeling, this first job. Then one day she witnesses a disturbing sight:

> I saw her open one [of the screened cupboards in which she kept the milk] and pour the milk out of a big dishpan. . . . Now this old lady had eight cats that lived on the back porch. . . . About five of [her cats] scrambled into the open safe and began lapping up the milk in the dishpan. . . . When she came back, she just let those cats help themselves. . . . I stood there and thought of how many times I had drunk that milk. "I'll starve before I eat any more of it" [swears Moody]. (40)

Moody's mother dismisses the girl's report, insisting that the white woman doesn't sell milk from which cats drank. Moody continues to bring the milk home to her family, but she will no longer touch it. The incident brings us back to slave narratives, in which African Americans were linked with domestic beasts; Frederick Douglass's description of little children eating at a trough like pigs is one example.[9] When Moody describes the episode of her family drinking the same stuff as the woman's cats, the white practice of seeing African Americans as animals is made clear.

Subsequently Moody finds gastronomic pleasure and commensality in the home of a different white employer. Mrs. Claiborne teaches home economics at the local white school. Moody loves her job "because I made almost as much as Mama," and because the Claibornes pay her enough to purchase sandwich bread for school lunches. Moody had refused to eat lunch publicly after being teased for her meals of peanut butter on homemade biscuits: "All day long I was hungry but it was better than being laughed at by my classmates" (39). As Moody had seen before, white families ate differently from her family. But this white woman did not merely provide a kind of shop window through which the girl could look at but not partake of the goodies. Instead, Mrs. Claiborne "taught me what a balanced meal was and how to set a table and how to cook foods we never ate at home. I'd never known anything about having meat, vegetables, and a salad. . . . I enjoyed learning about these things, not that they were helpful at our house" (41). Knives aren't needed if there's no meat. Poverty dictated beans and bread as staples at the Moody home, as it does in other American families to this day.

Sociologist Pierre Bourdieu has asserted that many people maintain a lifelong affection for the "foods that are simultaneously most 'filling' and most economical . . . [resulting in] . . . the taste of necessity."[10] But Moody never waxes nostalgic for the monotonous meals of her childhood. A taste for the food one eats when impoverished may in France be considered an "*amor fati,* the choice of destiny . . . a forced choice, produced by conditions of existence," but the racial context of the United States creates a different narrative.[11] Even as a child, Moody knows that white meals differed, and as she grows older she waits for the varied diet, like the salads described by Mrs. Claiborne, that will signal her freedom from racial hierarchy. If we judge by the intensity of Moody's recollections, it is hard to believe she would seek out an unadorned plate of beans or a peanut butter and biscuit sandwich as a way of recapturing her youthful days. Her past was not a series of halcyon events.

One Saturday, Mrs. Claiborne's husband asks the girl to join them at the dinner table. Abashed and shy, Moody says almost nothing and the family dines in near silence. By dessert, conversation has begun, and the guest reveals how well she does in school; at that point the Claibornes decide to host her for dinner every Saturday. In short: "They started treating me like their own child" (42). When Moody's family finally moves to a house built by her stepfather, the girl doesn't want to go; she would have to stop working for the Claibornes and miss out on the equality and good food shared. The backbreaking labor Moody endures the summer her stepfather tries farming combines synergistically with her memories of the conversations she had had with the Claibornes: "Whenever Mama started one of her long lectures about the pleasures of farming, I would drown her out with my thoughts of Mrs. Claiborne. . . . [She] had told me how smart I was and how much I could do if I just had a chance" (90). Regular meals with welcoming whites helped confirm Moody's beliefs.

If Moody's childhood deprivations and humiliations forged her spirit, other acts of eating—or not eating—fanned the flames of her righteous anger. Just before she begins high school, Chicago teenager Emmett Till is kidnapped, tortured, and murdered while visiting Mississippi relatives. Over the ever-present plate of beans the horrified adolescent asks her mother about the crime, the lowly meal underscoring their entrapment in the racist social order. Her mother sharply replies, "Don't you let on that you know nothing about that boy being killed before Mrs. Burke [Moody's latest after-school employer]" (130). Mrs. Burke, member of a Klan-like women's group, corners Moody in the kitchen, insinuating that if the girl forgets her place she will suffer Till's fate. Although Moody had been eating when she is accosted, she thinks, "[I] couldn't have eaten now if I were starving" (132). As she returns home, the teenager sees the connection between racism and hunger, reflecting that "now there was a new fear known to me—the fear of being killed just because I was black. . . . [With the fear of hunger] I knew once I got food, the fear of starving would leave" (132). Moody correctly identifies this new threat as monstrous, an irrational hatred with possibly fatal results. Subsequently, her homeroom teacher, noticing that the teenager is studying rather than eating during lunchtime, tries to draw her out. The sympathetic educator asks her student to tell her what's going on, and the two have dinner shortly afterward at the young woman's home. Commensality offers food for eating and food for thought, as Mrs. Rice not only talks to Moody about the Till murder but also about the NAACP: "You see the NAACP is doing a lot for Negroes in the South. I shouldn't be telling you this. And don't you dare breathe a word of what I said" (134). Moody "digested a good meal . . . and a whole new pool of knowledge" (135), which, like Frederick Douglass, she finds more precious than calories. Moody keeps her confidence, but at the end of the year the progressive teacher is fired.

A college dining hall serves as the place where the civil rights activist combines her education with activism. Natchez Junior College, which high school basketball star Moody attends, is a historically Black and underresourced institution. Given her employment experience, Moody goes to work in the kitchen, where she at first believes she will have some impact. Soon she "came to realize that there wasn't much you could do with baloney and potatoes, our two main dishes" (240). In her second year she leads the students in a strike over maggot-infested grits: after her friends point to the insects in their cereal, Moody marches into the kitchen pantry to find water dripping onto the shelves. Announcing, "We don't eat until he gets rid of Miss Harris [the head cook] and that leak is fixed!" Moody begins a rebellion (257). When the students ask how they will eat, Moody puts up half of her own savings and solicits funds from the male students; their home cooking fuels a week-long boycott. Although Natchez's president makes changes, Moody refuses—as she did with the incident of the clabber milk—to eat food she believes to be tainted. She finishes the year by eating the canned food her family sends her, and she is rewarded for her activism and academic persistence with a scholarship to Tougaloo (259–60).

Tougaloo was home to many civil rights activists, and fittingly the climax to Moody's education is not a commencement ceremony with family smiling from the sidelines. The emphatic punctuation mark to Moody's undergraduate career is provided by the 1963 Woolworth lunch counter sit-in. The retelling of this pivotal event takes up just a few pages of Moody's book (288–93). She sketches the action almost tersely, remembering her request to the waitress: "We would like to be served here." The waitress responds by turning out the lights behind the counter and fleeing. A couple of whites sitting at the counter get up and move away, but one girl finishes her ice cream sundae before leaving. An older woman expresses sympathy for Moody and her friends before she, too, departs. Once these patrons leave, a mob of white high school students arrives to shout epithets at Moody and fellow demonstrators (who include faculty from the college). The violent racists then start "smearing us with ketchup, mustard, sugar, pies, and everything on the counter" (289). The standoff comes to an end several hours later, after the nonviolent participants have been assaulted by hurled curses, thrown food, and vicious blows, despite the president of Tougaloo petitioning the police to protect the students. When the police eventually appear, they allow the enraged whites to continue throwing objects as the Tougaloo group exits the store. Of the aftermath, Moody reflects, "All I could think of was how sick Mississippi whites were. They believed so much in the segregated Southern way of life, they would kill to preserve it" (292). The explosion of violence eclipses Moody's college graduation. The author ends her narrative on a subdued note, suffering from shock and survivor's guilt: her encouragement helped draw a local businessman into the struggle, and he ends up on a chain gang with his livelihood destroyed.

Moody's autobiography casts her life and work in terms of too many meals denied and too few shared. Hers is a tale of "food abuse."[12] *Coming of Age in Mississippi* endures as a testimony to Moody's courage. As a historical document of contested commensalities, her narrative has few equals, affording an unusually detailed view of the way food functions as an exclusionary tool. Meals here are the stages on which the struggles for equality and dignity are fought. Moody knows that pitched battles are waged over the right to eat and the right to eat enough.

Like *Coming of Age in Mississippi*, food insecurity and the limited diet of the rural poor shape Alice Walker's *Meridian*.[13] While Meridian Hill, the eponymous heroine of Walker's novel, does not participate in a lunch counter protest, she, like Moody, experiences the dangers of interracial commensality through the fallout from a single diner meal. As Mark Weiner has observed, "the students who demonstrated at Woolworth stores across the South used the image of denied hamburgers and Cokes to urge citizens to greater sacrifice";[14] Moody, Walker, and their peers understood that American citizenship incongruously depends in part on equal access to cheap, unappetizing food. Pregnant and wed as a teenager, Meridian, energized by civil rights workers in her small town, leaves her husband and child to attend a historically Black women's college. On campus, she joins with other young activists. In the process she falls in love with Truman Held, a politically engaged young man. Like the real Anne Moody, the fictional Meridian is struck by the inequities she sees; even in her new circle she perceives class divisions. One night, after registering voters in a more rural area, Meridians's friends go out for a meal with other young people: Truman, whom she once loved; his white wife, Lynne Rabinowitz; and two Black fellow activists, Tommy Odds and Trilling. The food was nothing to savor: "At the Moonflower, a greasy hole-in-the-wall that still had 'Whites Only' on its door. . . . The food had been so bad they had not been able to eat it but they had left in high spirits" (141–42). The "Whites Only" sign underscored the triumph of ordering and eating at a segregated restaurant.

But their meal was no victory. Several days later, when Truman, Tommy, and another man are leaving a building, gunfire breaks out. The two men on either side of Tommy leap to safety, but the man in the middle goes down, shot through the elbow. Visiting his friend, Truman is shocked to find Tommy not just wounded, but an amputee. Understandably bitter, the mutilated man attacks Truman verbally, blaming the shooting and the loss of his arm on Truman's choice of wife. Lynne is as guilty as the sniper, the man in the hospital bed insists. They had all been seen eating together, inflaming the local vigilantes: "They shouldn't have done it, of course. They had been warned against it. They knew better" (141). Truman at first rejects this accusation, then he reflects: "Was it because she was a white woman that Lynne was guilty? Ah, yes. That was it" (141). Only then does Truman remember they had been followed from the diner, and that Lynne's appearance with Black men would have been inflammatory in the Deep South. By breaking taboos against miscegenation and eating in a "Whites Only" café, the group would trespass two terrains, inviting retaliatory violence. Once that first barrier against interracial commensality was breached, there was no safety anywhere in town.

Food and dining within a racially mixed context signals transgression and danger for minority group members, as we have already seen in *Coming of Age in Mississippi*. Struggles over commensality appear within minority groups, too. Although most critics of *Meridian* have discussed Lynne's whiteness, relatively fewer address her Jewish ethnicity. Lauren Cardon has argued that Walker was cognizant of the double bind that Jews were in: having only recently shed their nonwhite status, they risked losing "their experience of otherness that facilitates empathy."[15] Scenes in which the northern-raised Lynne encounters eastern European Jewish food show how specific foods can draw members in or lead to their rejection. For reasons she cannot articulate, Lynne occasionally shops at the Jewish delicatessen in their overwhelmingly Christian community. Even though "it was expensive and she had little money," she continues to go there, even after the owners would "fling the food at her . . . when she would come in with one, maybe two, black men, or women" (195). Interracial commensality was nearly as powerful a taboo for Jews as for Christians; separated by religion, the two groups were nevertheless putatively united by skin color. Racial prejudice is a sin for which Lynne cannot forgive her fellow Jews, with her enmity emerging in rhetoric linking identity with comestibles. When the counterman wordlessly signals that she should "return to the fold," she rejects his overtures; in an interior monologue she contemptuously calls him a "slicer of salami. [A] Baker of Challah!" (196). Her scorn, cast as disdain for Jewish foodstuffs, undercuts her seemingly en-lightened racial stance, for she herself reverts to stereotyping when angered. Sounding the internalized struggles of 1960s-era activists, Walker illustrates that tensions around and over food appear intraracially as well.

Lynne's angry response calls out Jews' false sense of security as "whites." When the local synagogue is bombed by anti-Semites, the deli is closed, with the owners expressing horror. Lynne is not surprised, as she knew Christian patronage would not protect the shop owners from religious hatred.[16] Lynne's revulsion in the shop expresses dismay and anger that her own folks, with their history of oppression, would adopt the prejudiced attitudes of the con-servative southern mainstream. Internalizing self-hate, she rejects pickles and challah as unappetizing—although they are items she returns to again and again—invoking their names as she would a curse word. The shared tastes of Jewish ethnicity pull activist and shopkeeper toward one another at the same time it pushes them apart. Walker knows that unless Lynne comes to terms with her contradictory feelings about her identity, she will be unable to grasp her role in the struggle for civil rights.[17] Understanding one's relationship to food can be key to forward movement.

Walker starts *Meridian* in the narrative present, a strategy well suited to unpacking the complexity of 1960s activism, often viewed reductively and retroactively as interracially united young people struggling against an older generation divided by hatred and fear. By opening the novel after most of the narrative action has taken place, Walker asks us to consider the continuing life of nonviolent action as a means of dismantling de facto segregation. Tru-man—older, single again, once more in love with Meridian—has found her staging a protest against segregated admission policies for a traveling side-show. After a tense standoff with a decommissioned tank, Meridian carries the day before collapsing in exhaustion and being carried home by supporters. Truman ponders her ill health, for although she lives in a sparsely furnished home, she is surrounded by comestibles: "Ever since I've been here people have been bringing boxes and boxes of food. Your house is packed with stuff to eat" (11). Meridian replies that her neighbors are grateful that she has volunteered to suffer in their stead; to thank her, they feed her, even bringing her a cow to milk. Food freely offered bridges the gap between white and Black, as well as between the college student and the poorly educated. Wracked by an unnamed illness, Meridian nevertheless continues to put her life on the line for principle. Walker underscores the isolation of the outsider in the small-town South: the Black folks of Chicokema admire and feed her but keep their distance from "that weird gal that strolled into town last year" (6). Meridian remains a valued outsider, one who eats by herself but is provisioned by her neighbors.

After we have seen Meridian attend college and work with fellow activists Black and white, northern and southern; after Martin Luther King Jr. is assassinated; after she settles in Chicokema, Truman accompanies Meridian to a dilapidated house, where a young mother lays dying. Wanting only her last loving looks at her husband and child and to be buried on Mother's Day, the woman chats with Meridian about getting laid off from her factory job and the venison stew her husband Johnny is cooking. Unemployed, her young man rolls discarded, food-soiled newspapers into "logs," selling them for pennies as fuel—"a nickel apiece and to colored only three pennies" (224). Meridian joins in the dirty work while advocating voter registration. He refuses the invitation, invoking his mortally ill wife and their shoeless son as the necessity of earning what little he can without jeopardy. Meridian accepts his response but, after briefly leaving the house, returns with two bags of groceries. Although we see him peering doubtfully into the sacks, "after Mother's Day" he brings over ten logs and a half dozen freshly skinned rabbits—then signs up to be registered to vote (226). Simply, Walker illustrates the power of shared food to bring confidence and change alike. Contested, offered, or accepted, meals in *Meridian* point the way to dignity and equality before the law.

Ernest Gaines's *A Gathering of Old Men* has no scene of violence-inspiring commensality, nor does it focus on eating together or dining apart.[18] For Gaines, born in the decade prior to Moody and Walker but, like them, the child of sharecroppers, the pen seemed as effective as a sword in the fight to register voters or teach in freedom schools. Gaines chronicled the 1960s in rural Louisiana, where the scenes he depicts, absent specific details such as automobiles, could have been set in the late nineteenth century. Gaines believed his contributions to civil rights activism could best be made in writing. John Lowe has observed that "when [Gaines] was asked to march, he decided he would go back to his room and try to write the best sentence he could that day that would speak to the issues."[19] For his part Herman Beavers sees Gaines "recuperat[ing] the South as a site, not only of expressive culture, but also of African American resistance. This resistance takes many forms . . . [that are] difficult to categorize and impossible to elude."[20] In Gaines's fictionalized Louisiana, a shot of liquor taken in a cabin, a withheld pie, and a basket of sandwiches reveal the slowly changing attitudes of whites.

Gathering's narrative tension derives from a day-long cascade of events, set off by the shooting of a white farmer by a Black farmhand. Gaines shifts point of view throughout the novel, from the perspective of African American laborers to that of privileged whites. Readers first meet the members of a large cast at a dinner table. Formerly known as the boy Snookum, the adult narrator recalls the "gathering" day, when his childish pell-mell run sounded a community alarm.[21] He and two other children were at table: "Gram Mom was at the stove looking in the pot to see if she had enough food left in there for supper" (3). What they have, and plenty of, is turnips. When one child complains, "I isn't no turnip eating machine," the grandmother sharply replies that he'd better turn into one (4). Told to spread the word about the killing, Snookum takes off running and avoids the root vegetable stew. At his first stop Snookum asks Janey, a Black cook, for a tasty reward: "You getting me some tea cakes, or a plarine?" (9).[22] Horrified at the news, the older woman walks off to alert others, leaving Snookum empty handed. His witness of the dead man's body will have to stand in for the desired payment, for while he may have to return to turnips, he still has something over the other children.

Foodways figure prominently in Gaines's writerly toolkit as do his numerous narrators. Both portray the enforced taste of poverty and the boundaries drawn between groups. Courtney Ramsay has observed that Gaines's fiction "underlines the central significance of foodways as powerful symbols in [Louisiana] culture."[23] While Snookum's dash to rally the elders of his community provides a kind of comic relief, regionally specific foods arouse the reader's emotions: few children would willingly substitute cooked turnips for pralines.

"Amused" is not the word that comes to mind for the remainder of the story. *Gathering*'s catalytic event, the shooting in self-defense of a white man by a Black man, would historically have led to a "necktie party" (73), not a picnic. Strangely, the killing also occasions a revelation of interracial respect enacted around commensality. When an assortment of African American men claim credit for the killing to protect one of their own, the white sheriff,

Mapes, demands that the charade come to an end. Mapes assumes that Mathu, an older but still physically powerful Black man on whose property the shooting took place, pulled the trigger. The sheriff's high opinion of Mathu—even though he is Black—leads him to this interpretation. Embodying a certain style of southern masculinity, the sheriff scorns any men who do not fit the mold: "Mapes was . . . big, mean, brutal. But Mapes respected a man. Mathu was a man, and Mapes respected Mathu. But he didn't think much of the rest of us, and he didn't respect us."[24] Mapes's uncommon respect for Mathu is apparent: "Mapes liked Mathu. They had hunted together. . . . And Mapes had had a few drinks with Mathu at Mathu's house. He *liked* Mathu" (84, my emphasis). Levels of tolerance and intimacy between individuals can be gauged by whether they drink or dine together.[25] Viewed from the perspective of hospitality, American mealtime boundaries signal levels of respect that do not necessarily translate into beliefs in equality. Mapes and Mathu have never eaten together, attesting to the unseen racial barriers that become visible once we bring food, literally and figuratively, to the table. Yet when Gaines describes the two men, one white and one Black, as having shared a drink, he suggests that social chasms may in time be bridged: as Mary Douglas has observed, "There is no reason to suppose [such boundaries] will always matter."[26]

When food is shared and eaten, cultural boundaries are crossed, even if the racial distinctions aren't erased. Gaines sets a pivotal scene around a basket of sandwiches: Miss Merle, the white woman who helped raise Candy Marshall (who set into motion the gathering to save Mathu, who in turn helped raise her), de-escalates the rising tension with a simple offering. Right before she enters the picture, the dead man's younger brother had appeared, demanding answers. This younger man, one-half of a pair of star high school football players (one white, one Black) known as Salt and Pepper, embodies the "new" Louisiana; the deceased, a harsh employer of Black workers, represents the old order. After the teenager storms out, a lull falls over the assembled: each of the players at Mathu's hangs in suspended animation, waiting for something to happen. It is at this point Miss Merle arrives, carrying a basket of wrapped sandwiches, and begins to distribute them. As Candy's boyfriend recalls, "I suppose she felt that since we were all conspirators together, one was no better than the others, so she just started dishing out sandwiches to the first person she got to, and fussing all the time. . . . 'I hope you like ham and cheese, because there isn't anything else' [said Miss Merle]." Standing by her with his gun drawn, the sheriff's assistant draws Miss Merle's ire: "Can't you put that thing away for a second? . . . Who are you going to shoot, the hog?" (125–26). Moving around him, she passes out sandwiches "neatly wrapped in wax paper [with] lettuce and tomatoes on the ham and cheese." Although Miss Merle continually mutters, "Just look at that" at nothing in particular, everyone gets fed: "No one there was not eating. Mapes, Candy, Mathu, Griffin, the old men, the old women, the children—everybody was eating. We were all hungry" (126). Snookum, who would not eat his turnips and begged for a sweet, is the first to ask for seconds. Miss Merle looks down at the boy, a "dusty" and "grimy" little kid, and "doesn't want to feel pity"; to express that emotion would mean to feel for the others and jeopardize her own worldview. What she does is give him a second sandwich, at the same time shooing him off ("Now, get away from me") (127). To mask her rising empathy, she must wave him away like a mosquito, but the care she has taken with the food delivers another message.

Despite their hunger, others who would like seconds turn them down, as there are not enough sandwiches for everyone to have two. Miss Merle mutters that she did not have enough in her larder to make more. When sandwiches remain after the basket is passed around a second time, she simply presses what's left on "the different people who looked hungriest to her." Then there is another round of apologies: because the pie she has at home is not large enough to give a slice to all, no one will get dessert (128). When Mapes gives his thanks, Candy's boyfriend notices that Miss Merle seems as ready to knock everyone down with the empty basket as she is to accept their appreciation. Against the convictions and conventions of race and class, Miss Merle offered food to all present, Black and white. Her inner compass refuses to allow inherited ideologies to dictate whom she will feed and how. Even after a killing, and on the precipice of a racial abyss, the human desire for commensality, Gaines suggests, sometimes gets the upper hand.

As individuals who lived through the 1960s, Moody, Gaines, and Walker, tackled bigotry and its erasure through direct action and as authors. The metaphors and symbolic action of foodways—diners, meals, food insecurity—enabled them to show that the struggle for American civil rights takes place in arenas even more ordinary than voting booths and picket lines. Food is a field of action: the kitchens, dining rooms, and restaurants of the southern United States tell us as much. Sometimes progress can be had at the counter of a five-and-dime; sometimes we find it in a pile of neatly wrapped sandwiches.

The Signifying Dish

Autobiography and History in Two Black Women's Cookbooks

The image of the Black woman cook—overweight, decked out in a snowy apron, undisputed genius of the American kitchen—is indelibly inscribed on the collective American unconscious. The late John Egerton concisely described this deep-rooted stereotype:

> They [Black women chefs] were "turbaned mammies" and "voodoo magicians" and "tyrants" who ruled the back rooms with simpleminded power; they could work culinary miracles day in and day out, but couldn't for the life of them tell anyone how they did it. Their most impressive dishes were described as "accidental" rather than planned. Their speech, humorously conveyed in demeaning dialect in many an old cookbook, came across as illiterate folk knowledge and not to be taken seriously.[1]

These buffoonish characters were the fictive counterparts of legions of unknown culinary workers—African Americans whose legacy and labor shaped much of what we eat to this day.[2] The stereotype of the mammy-cook continues to overshadow the historical presence of actual Black chefs.[3] As folklorist Patricia Turner asks, "What price has been exacted from the real black women who have been forced to make their way in a culture that pays homage to a distorted icon?"[4] This disjunction—between the spurious worship of an unlettered genius Black cook and that figure's long absence within what I call the "kitchens of power" led to Quandra Prettyman's 1992 inquiry: if "Black cooks are familiar figures in our national mythology as well as in our national history . . . [why is it] so few have produced cookbooks"?[5] And, although the number of Black-authored cookbooks has markedly increased, the question remains: How does one write a cookbook that engages with the shadows of Black slavery, the persistence of stereotypes and oppression, and the practicalities of cooking?[6]

To write and to cook—to participate in a national discourse about food and eating—leads the twentieth-century Black woman into a rhetorical minefield: to identify publicly as a cook means engaging with the ghosts and realities of American racism. Along with producing recipes, she must tackle visceral images with metaphor, individual agency, and historical memory. When writing about specific foods, the Black woman cook must always engage with these sites of memory, or *lieux des mémoires*, the places around which recalled lives and events circulate and people create significance.[7] Each recalled or recreated community dish signifies mightily, and the multiple readings of a simple meal of rice, greens, and meat reveal past and present. Race and culture define our national taste buds. In this layering of food and culture lies the quandary of the Black woman who would write a cookbook: Even if Aunt Jemima's image on the pancake mix box has been updated from kerchief-wearing mammy to trim working mother, has the consciousness of American consumers been similarly revised? Black women cooks haunt the African American female chef or author. In writing a recipe, can the Black woman cook also right history?

Following the crest of the Black Power movement, several works took on the figure of the Black woman cook and her problematic heritage. Vertamae Smart-Grosvenor's *Vibration Cooking, or Travel Notes of a Geechee Girl* (1970) and Carole and Norma Jean Darden's *Spoonbread and Strawberry Wine* (1978) quickly gained, and have retained, a loyal fan base.[8] Operating on gastronomic and historical levels alike, these volumes help us understand how a recipe collection embodies a personal and/or communal identity; each text works as autobiography and history while engaging linked issues of Black stereotyping and class. They illustrate the ways Black culinary traditions can be imagined or inscribed—whether by the author or her readers—to enact the cultural, expressive, and historical agenda of the African American female. Along with how-tos, the Dardens and Smart-Grosvenor give us whys, enacting a culinary Black Reconstruction.

As we now know, the first published cookbooks by Black women appeared a century before: Malinda Russell's in 1866, and Abby Fisher's in 1881. Amid the culinary instruction typical of a cookbook, the authors' personal lives and historical contexts emerge: Russell directly addresses the history of slavery in her own family, while Fisher's references to servitude can almost go unnoticed. Very few cookbooks bearing a Black woman's name as author appeared for decades, and those that did rarely strayed far from culinary matters.[9] Beginning in the 1940s, however, cookbooks started to recover and commemorate an African American culinary past. Freda DeKnight's *The Ebony Cookbook*, published in 1962, revised her *A Date With a Dish: A Cookbook of American Negro Recipes* (1948), about the same time the National Council of Negro Women sponsored a number of culinary celebrations of community, beginning in 1958 with the *Historical Cookbook of the American Negro*.[10] In the second half of the twentieth century, authors increasingly found food, politics, and history hard to disentangle.[11] The civil rights movement that began in the 1950s drove massive civil disobedience, with notable battles waged around access to food, followed by the call for Black Power and Black Arts in the 1960s and 1970s. With this surge came a burgeoning market for Black subjects, and the growing numbers of African American–owned presses after 1960 attest to the demand for books by and about Black peoples.[12] A number of African American cookbooks followed. Volumes such as *A Good Heart and Light Hand* (1968) explored and celebrated African American identity through relatively straightforward collections of recipes.[13] These movements and books paved the way for the Dardens and Smart-Grosvenor, who engagingly reflected the creative and political consciousness of the 1960s.

Smart-Grosvenor, a South Carolina–born actress, musician, and writer, personified Black Power's sass. With the opening remarks of *Vibration*, she unequivocally asserts that, for too long, Caucasians have been dictating who's in charge of the American kitchen: "White folks act like they invented food and like there is some weird mystique surrounding it—something that only Julia [Child] and Jim [James Beard] can get to. There is no mystique. Food is food. Everybody eats!" (3). Her leveling observation proclaims that a single group does not own American cuisine. The Darden sisters also inform their reader-cooks that the legacy of slavery and racism affects the foods we remember: Despite contacting numerous family members, the Dardens "could not trace [their] family roots past [their] grandparents. . . . Such was the effect of slavery and its resulting destruction of family ties" (xi). The Dardens and Smart-Grosvenor similarly weave a love of cooking and eating around the markers of slavery, family pride, and the civil rights movement, but the differences between their cookbooks demonstrate generational shifts and class divisions within the Black community that became marked by the end of the twentieth century. While the Dardens showcase the elegant side of southern cuisine and more formal cooking styles, Smart-Grosvenor's folksy tone and simplified recipes seem to privilege classic soul food.[14] Together these women demonstrate that African America was, by the 1970s, increasingly diversified in terms of class, educational achievement, and region.[15]

In a society long arranged around binaries of white and Black, free and slave, middle and upper class, African Americans continue to be seen as exceptional. Because of the persistent linkage between race and economic status in the United States, Black women—with their history of slavery and low-wage work—and their culinary creations were often viewed as less refined than their European counterparts.[16] The very existence of a cookbook, an object often assumed to be a feminine universal, obscures class issues for cookbooks are as stratified by socioeconomic station, region, and ideology as the women who write them. For many years the majority of African Americans were working class and so less likely to write, compile, or even read recipe books; the exigencies of work and their financial situation militated against leisure activities such as gourmet cooking.[17] Nevertheless, because of their presence within multiple culinary systems—mainstream (or "white") and culturally specific (or "Black")—Black women cooks created and create in a heterogeneous culinary system.

The Dardens and Smart-Grosvenor recognize that there is neither a monolithic Black culture nor a single African American cuisine. Each of their books plays up and against prevalent notions of what "Black" food is and is not. Their subtitles reveal distinctive agendas—*Spoonbread and Strawberry Wine: Recipes and Reminiscences of a Family* invites us into a procession of middle-class homes to sample fruit wines, hot baked goods, and comfortable living; family photographs underscore this cuisine's traditional bent. *Vibration Cooking, or, the Travel Notes of a Geechee Girl* announces the author's unorthodox but down-home approach: putting together tradition and intuition, a global roster of recipes showcase picaresque adventures in the rural South, New York City, Paris, and Cuba, to name a few of the places invoked.[18] The Dardens present a gastronomic social history of African America, emphasizing nineteenth- and early twentieth-century ideals of racial uplift in the face of adversity. As Anne Goldman commented, "If the Dardens are intent on providing their own middle-class status with an historical precedent, they are equally interested in providing ignorant readers with lessons in nineteenth-century American history."[19] For her part, Smart-Grosvenor offers an idiosyncratic, wisecracking personal narrative of the changes under way in 1970s Black America. If *Spoonbread*'s text with its sepia-toned pictures can be called a loving archive, then the immediacy of *Vibration Cooking*'s plainspoken first-person narrative creates a Black Arts gastronomy. Each set of culinary reminiscences captures a moment in African American history. While *Spoonbread* can at times seem like an idealization of the past—segregation had its positive sides in the enforced closeness of Black community life is one sentiment that comes to mind—*Vibration Cooking*'s author comes across like a Zora Neale Hurston of the culinary set.[20] By the late 1970s, desegregation had been achieved—at least as far as the courts were concerned—and increasing numbers of African Americans entered the enclaves of formerly all-white institutions. *Spoonbread* and *Vibration Cooking* can therefore be seen as late twentieth-century Black cultural events, expressions of the prevailing winds of change.

Vibration Cooking, the first published of the two books, came as a high-water mark at the nexus of Black Power and cuisine.[21] Smart-Grosvenor consciously counterwrites those generations-old images of portly Black geniuses who presided over generations of southern kitchens with nary a written recipe.[22] Before offering any recipes of her own, the author engages pointedly with prevailing myths, when she dedicates her work "to my mama and my grandmothers and my sisters in appreciation of the years that they worked in miss ann's kitchen and then came home to TCB in spite of slavery and oppression and the moynihan report" (v).[23] Smart-Grosvenor's recipes, related in a contemporary African American vernacular, place the cook within the community of Black women who like to whip things up—for themselves, for their families, for their lovers. These recipes are not for Miss Ann's kitchen: cooking as domestic service is invoked only to be scorned. (Despite the supposed bonds of sisterhood, women of different races and classes do not easily fall into sisterhood in the kitchen.) Smart-Grosvenor liberates the Black female cooks pigeonholed by the mainstream through scathing commentary, humor, and a very personal take on history.[24]

Vibration Cooking aims to eradicate culinary racism along with other kinds of bigotry. In the introduction, titled "The Demystification of Food," Smart-Grosvenor writes: "In reading lots and lots of cookbooks written by white folks it occurred to me that people very casually say Spanish rice, French fries, Italian spaghetti, Chinese cabbage. . . . With the exception of black bottom pie and niggertoes [Brazil nuts], there is no reference to black people's contributions to the culinary arts" (3). The introduction to the second edition extends the critique to tell us that "the white folks were on my case" about the original edition of *Vibration Cooking*. She expected mainstream readers to be puzzled by her frank mixing of culinary and political motives. Her cookbook, which includes a running commentary on Black life in the white United States, calls out "the segregation of ethnic foods in supermarkets. . . . Why can't the mango juice be with the tomato juice . . . [and not in] some 'exotic' section" (197)? She also includes an entire chapter about the Black person's inability to hail a taxicab in Manhattan—something New Yorkers still experience (95–97). Smart-Grosvenor called it like she saw it. In the text preceding a recipe for her paternal uncle's corn muffins, Smart-Grosvenor's readers learn why her father was called "a bad nigger" by a southern white, and how a racial slur might sometimes be a left-handed compliment (42–43). In another chapter, she enumerates "Name-Calling," the culinary imperialism inherent in the renaming of foods such as okra (the original African word is *gombo*) or succotash (she prefers a transliterated Native American spelling, *sukquttash*). Although she adds a recipe for "Cracker Stew," whose ingredients perform a veritable culinary dozens, Smart-Grosvenor admits she does not generally "call people out of their name" (85). Her disdain for things "white" has to be complicated, for as an African American she cannot simply dismiss European culture. Instead, when and wherever possible, she asserts the superiority of the African or Black influence.

That desire to refocus American gastronomic history leads Smart-Grosvenor to invoke and then discard the legacy of expatriate American cookbook author and memoirist Alice B. Toklas.[25] Both women can be termed unconventional, as they each lived in defiance of white middle-class American heteronormative culture. Toklas was a lesbian whose lifelong partner was the writer Gertrude Stein; Smart-Grosvenor was a Black American who refused to be channeled into either the stuffy respectability of the American Negro middle class or the still-segregated bohemian life of the American abroad. When Smart-Grosvenor mimics her supposed readers, asking, "Was I trying to be a black Alice B. Toklas?" she snaps, "The only thing I have in common with Alice B. Toklas is that we lived on the same street in Paris [the rue des Fleurus]. I lived at #17 and she at #27" (xvi). That she knows just where Toklas lived makes the comparison between them unavoidable: as American expatriates in Paris, Smart-Grosvenor and Toklas each record in their books a smart set of renowned visitors and their amusing anecdotes. Despite their differences in social class, both women moved in a vigorous and exhilarating artistic community.[26] While Toklas's text often included the *bon mots* of Gertrude Stein, Smart-Grosvenor never alludes directly to her husband or any other long-term partner. She records her own witticisms and observations as well as those of her children, Chandra and Kali: "My daughter said, 'My mamma cook like Aretha Franklin sing!'" (xv). Her sense of worth does not increase by simply being an observer of the greats (and near-greats) of American cultural history.[27] Yet both *Vibration* and the Toklas volume—in drawing connections between gastronomy and the arts—invite readers to be impressed by the authors' creative networks. Recipes in both books celebrate artists of all sorts—novelists, "Chicken Carlene Polite" (*Vibration* 165); painters, "Oeufs Francis Picabia" (*Toklas* 30); composer Virgil Thomson contributes a recipe for "shad roe mousse" to Toklas's book (230) while shoe designer Donald Hubbard worries about a "soul food party . . . in Rome" in *Vibration* (74).[28]

Smart-Grosvenor's reluctance to admit kinship with Toklas attests to her stronger desire to form a chain of Black women forebears.[29] The Geechee girl frankly seeks out connections with the women of the African diaspora, from whom she draws courage and inspiration.[30] When she introduces a "white" dish and then replaces it with a "Black" analog, Smart-Grosvenor performs a Black female signifying (or, she might say, a "hurting") on white gourmet foods: her comparisons of crepes with her grandmother's hoe cakes and "Pancakes Smith St. Jacques" exemplify this culinary revisionism (22, 23). In her preface to the 1986 edition, those who have come and cooked before her such as Edna Lewis and Ruth Gaskins receive high praise; so too does she compliment the famous, if less self-consciously aesthetic, Freda DeKnight.[31] A scandalized Smart-Grosvenor notes that few cookbooks by African Americans appeared before the first edition of *Vibration*—this despite the fact that "Afro-American cooking is like jazz—a genuine art form that deserves serious scholarship" (xviii).[32] Her assertion that cooking merits scholarly attention, like other forms of nonwritten artistic expression, anticipated scholarship in African American, women's, and cultural studies. Even so, the multiple genres of *Vibration Cooking*—epistolary, gastronomic, autobiographical— assert Smart-Grosvenor's agenda to be personal rather than academic.

In *Spoonbread and Strawberry Wine*, the Darden sisters make their cooking less autobiographical and more historical. If the welter of different texts offered by Smart-Grosvenor presents her recipes in the context of an individual's unique life experiences, the carefully researched and kitchen-tested recipes of several generations of Dardens and Sampsons attest to the conviction that the individual is inextricable from the larger community of Black folks.[33] So, when a friend of the two sisters inquires, "Didn't their black American *family*, deeply rooted in the experiences of slavery and rural life, have rich material on genuine American cookery?" the sisters answer yes (ix, my emphasis). Realizing that many of the dishes they "had taken for granted" were more real to them than the relatives dispersed across generations and regions, the two decided to put together a cookbook. For these sisters, a compendium of beloved foods would be inextricable from recapturing past African American life; compiling them properly would result in a "thick description" of a past age.[34] *Spoonbread* presents "a testimonial to those who lovingly fed us and at the same time gave us a better sense of ourselves by sharing themselves" (xi). Ingested along with those earliest bites was their African American identity.[35] Northern-raised and Sarah Lawrence–educated, the two sisters travel south to visit distant relatives and recapture their culinary and familial antecedents, specifically referring to their journey as "our pilgrimage 'home'" (xi). They visit neighbors in small towns, pick through boxes of photographs, and collect, try out, and standardize old recipe cards. Statements from historical personages abound in *Spoonbread*, although these figures from the past are surviving relatives and old friends of the family. Rather than Smart-Grosvenor's savory stew of recipes, letters from friends, and anecdotes about hobnobbing in the bohemian Black Arts world, the Dardens recreate, course by formal course, a lived experience they see vanishing with increased social mobility, desegregation, and distance from slavery. Theirs is not an autobiography composed of individual cooking stories (although some are included). It is in the number of recipes culled from older relatives, set down with those contributed by the Dardens, that we see where the emphasis in *Spoonbread* lies. As the youngest contributors, the Dardens subsume their culinary stories within a larger narrative of their maternal and paternal ancestors. With their own recollected meals the Darden sisters place themselves within the continuum of African American history.

By mapping out each side of their family and giving credit for each recipe where due, the sisters acknowledge that there is no single Black cuisine. Each branch of the Sampsons and the Dardens is identified, and every chapter refers to a specific family member. Accompanying photographs and reminiscences heighten the succulence and significance of the recipes within. Following a brief biography of the only grandparent they ever knew, adaptations of granddad Sampson's honey-based recipes follow: "Fruited Honey Chicken," "Honey Duck," "Honey Custard," even "Cough Syrup" (148–51). Memories of girlhood travels in the segregated South precede a picnic menu with "Hot Crab Meat

Salad" and "Edna Neil's Pan-fried Blowfish," the dishes of friends who provided food and shelter (248, 249).

Many of those whose recipes are included, or to whom chapters are dedicated, were elderly or deceased at the time of the writing, lending *Spoonbread* an elegiac tone. Although not quite a eulogy for a vanished African America, *Spoonbread* strikes a nostalgic note absent from *Vibration Cooking*.[36] "Thoughts of [our uncle] J. B. conjure up images of big shiny cars, polished two-toned shoes, straw hats tipped to the side, and the continual party that always seemed to be going on around him. . . . He was a cook [who] . . . preferred to eat his 'dinner' first thing in the morning" (53). The wistful tone could almost suggest that *Spoonbread* was aimed at those who attended northern or integrated schools and grew up away from an extended Black family. Segregation of a different kind remains, leaving the poorest African Americans almost as insulated from the middle-class Black world as the two races had once been. That separation informs a key agenda of these cookbooks: along with the invocation of time past or the articulation of a radical manifesto, *Spoonbread and Strawberry Wine* and *Vibration Cooking* offer specific remedies and recourse for those readers yearning to strengthen African American community through gastronomic venues. Their recipes and remembrances look to the past to forge a modern Black identity.[37]

But what of those with neither the time nor the wherewithal to prepare the classic, labor-intensive dishes of African American cuisine? Working parents with attenuated links to an older generation might just as soon purchase precooked African American food as prepare it themselves; those home-cooked Sunday meals are disappearing, too.[38] The owner of an Atlanta chain of drive-in chitlins restaurants asserted that "doctors, lawyers, all kinds of people . . . remember" this and other foods of their youth and came to buy them.[39] Others with "the yearning for collard or turnip greens" can now "pick a few cans off the [supermarket] shelf," for Black culinary culture is now available in a can.[40] Such convenience food businesses thrive in part not just because busy people appreciate the convenience of prepared foods, but also because growing numbers of African Americans no longer know how, or even want, to cook like their elders. Many in contemporary Black America have no desire to eat foods such as offal, identified with past privation, saying: "I don't know what they are, but they're something nasty."[41] Just as older women turned away from the stereotypes of the Black cook, younger African Americans may eschew meals associated with the impoverished circumstances that led folks to eat "everything but the squeal."⁴² Those with the hankering for the occasional foray into heritage cooking can peruse *Spoonbread* and *Vibration Cooking*—books almost with the status of brand names.⁴³

The Dardens and Smart-Grosvenor know that to provide their readers with a handbook to Black community and cuisine they must include a discussion of hoppin' John, the New Year holiday's signature soul food dish. (New Year's expressions of African American identity date back to the early nineteenth century.)⁴⁴ Tradition holds that the homely dish of hoppin' John was named after a limping New Orleans slave who sold the dish or perhaps the children who hopped around the table begging for a taste; its origins are certainly diasporic.⁴⁵ The making of this plain fare sends the Dardens and Smart-Grosvenor down parallel memory lanes; the two sisters tell us that "on New Year's Day we always have Open House at our father's home. It is a leisurely day, designed to give us an opportunity to unwind from the frenzy of New Year's Eve. . . . Black folklore has it that hoppin' john brings good luck in the coming year, so we always serve this . . . essential" (223). Here, the Dardens link food, history, and folklore. By placing their hoppin' John, which they subtitle "Black Eyed Peas and Rice," in the context of Black American culture, and providing a precise ingredient list and step-by-step instructions, the Dardens attempt to ensure that their readers' gastronomic revivals of African American traditions will turn out successfully.

Smart-Grosvenor also connects black-eyed peas and rice to New Year's Day, although the link she forges does not lean on folklore or family:

[I remember] those New Year's open houses I used to have and everyone I loved would come. Even Millie came from Germany one year. She arrived just in time for the black eyes and rice. And that year I cooked the peas with beef neck bones instead of swine cause so many brothers and sisters have given up swine. I had ham hocks on the side for the others. . . . If you eat black-eyed peas and rice (Hopping John) on New Year's Day, you supposed to have good luck for the coming year. Black people been eating that traditional New Year's Day dinner for years. That's why I'm not having no more open house on New Year's Day. I'm going to try something new. (5, 6)

Strict adherence to tradition should not overrule the spirit of the occasion. Accordingly, Smart-Grosvenor's recipe runs four lines long:

Cook black-eyed peas.

When they are almost done add rice.
Mix rice and peas together.
Season and—voila!—you got it. (6)

So, although she gives us a recipe for hoppin' John, Smart-Grosvenor prefaces it with her explanation of why she omits the pork (because the prevailing Black ethos eschewed pig meat as the food of poverty, as well as revolting to our Muslim brothers and sisters), leaves the seasoning up to her audience (because we should cook by vibration), and intimates that she plans to skip it entirely on subsequent "firsts" (because she won't be bound by the past). Smart-Grosvenor nods to continuity, promotes the cook's own sense of integrity, and fosters innovation.[46] Still, some traditions must remain: nothing so newfangled as Teflon "can't fry no fried chicken" (4). For this cook, only the cast iron pots of her girlhood will do.[47]

The Dardens and Smart-Grosvenor must also address greens, that essential of the Black dinner plate. A colleague of mine once snapped, "Who ever thought 'African American food' was 'just grits and greens' anyway?" Although there may be some who still believe African Americans subsist largely on cornmeal and well-done vegetables, that bit of testiness speaks to intragroup notions about the food of rural Black southerners and urban Black northerners, as well as the Dardens' or Smart-Grosvenor's implied readership. To deny that such items were common mealtime offerings, and the legacy of generations of pinched food budgets, is to deny the past. More problematically, it also denies a link with the continent: Smart-Grosvenor knew as much, calling her second cookbook *Black Atlantic Cooking*.[48] To say greens are a cornerstone of Black cuisine doesn't limit the dish to a single tradition within that diaspora. As identified by Schomburg in the 1920s and again by Jessica B. Harris in the 1990s, there existed two "major African-American culinary traditions . . . that of the dirt-poor, hardscrabble Deep South . . . [and the one that] harked back to the kitchens of Virginia plantations manned by house slaves who turned spits, put up preserves, and served elegant meals." Both traditions consider cooked greens a standard dish.[49] The eating of collards has meanings analogous to endive or parsley on a Seder plate: for Jews and Blacks alike, the ingestion of bitter greens serves as a near literal taste of slavery and oppression. Shared food signals a shared identity, if not always a shared fate. Ironically, sometimes triumphantly, what we have to eat we sometimes come to prefer.[50]

For most African Americans, greens have a content beyond B vitamins and iron. Culinary historian Jessica Harris attests to their foundational status, noting that "Greens are undeniably one of the United States' best known African inspired foods"; they "go into the pot boiling on the back of the stove in a traditional Black American household."[51] Under "greens" the Dardens offer their readers three dishes: Mixed Greens, Collard Greens, and "Pot Likker," the liquid left after cooking the vegetable. Because their father "eats greens every day . . . [and] always makes them in quantity and reheats them during the week" (136), their recipes yield between twelve and sixteen servings. By not reducing the serving size, the sisters implicitly affirm the central place of cooked greens in Black American cuisine. Praising the value of pot likker, the sisters point out that "it is renowned for its nutritional value and can be used as an excellent vegetable stock for soups, as a soup in its own right, or traditionally to dunk corn bread" (137).[52] Provider of vitamins and representative of folk custom, greens serve as side dish and symbol.

Smart-Grosvenor celebrates nutrition and nationalism via greens. She emphatically asserts their classic heritage: "According to the National Geographic [they are] . . . prehistoric. The Romans took them to France and England. The Romans are said to have considered them a delicacy. I know I consider them a delicacy. They are very rich in minerals and vitamins" (139). When shopping in her Lower East Side Manhattan neighborhood, Smart-Grosvenor has an unpleasant déjà vu when the person of color wrapping her greens does not also take her money. That day a Puerto Rican man bundles her purchases; in her childhood it was a Black man who did that work. She vows to shop henceforth in Harlem for her greens, even if that means a subway ride uptown (141). Another day, when a white shopper asks "How do you people fix these?" the author declares that Blacks make salad with collards using "Italian" dressing. Nearby, "a black woman . . . looked at me as if I had discredited the race" (xvii).[53] With eleven recipes offered for these vegetable staples, *Vibration Cooking* affirms the tastiness, curative powers, and unshakable place of greens in Black American life.

Prepared year in and year out, soul food has nevertheless changed over time.[54] What we think of as African American cuisine persists, however, and while the boundaries of culinary Black America may alter, the category itself remains identifiable.[55] Foodways remain one of the strongest factors in group identity, for our earliest tastes set the stage for group belonging.[56] Eating "Black" determines an individual's cultural connection—all the more reason, as the African American community becomes more stratified, that the Dardens and Smart-Grosvenor take up the task of recreating a primal gastronomic identity.

Eating cannot be separated from personal, literary, or social identity; neither can you separate specific dishes from their historical context. When the Dardens describe the box lunches with which they and other Black Americans traveled, the accompanying recipes demand we acknowledge the Jim Crow transportation and hotel industry, which barred African Americans from public eating places and restricted their movement on common carriers (245–46). Smart-Grosvenor's own culinary history aims to return the Black past to its actors: outraged by white author William Styron's revisionist novel about insurrectionist Nat Turner, in which "Nat's last meal [was] roast pork and apple brandy," she creates a new recipe, "Nat Turner Apple Pork Thing" (182–83). If the Dardens' book acts as a gastronomic museum, Smart-Grosvenor's culinary autobiography regards modern Black cookery as an agent of change.[57] Smart-Grosvenor writes almost exclusively of her own life and the place food and cooking hold within it; the Dardens record the manner in which their mother, father, and older relatives ate. While these two Black cookbooks differ remarkably, their authors approach from complementary angles the "stuff" of African American culture. Each book places African American cuisine in a political context, records a social history that must not be forgotten, and relates the lived experience of the writer and her family.[58] Very much more than grits and greens, the dishes of the Dardens and Smart-Grosvenor signify mightily.

Elegy or *Sankofa*?

Edna Lewis's *Taste of Country Cooking*
and the Question of Genre

Cookbooks, as we have seen, must be thought of as more than collections of instructions for individual dishes and meals. But if food has long been well studied, the same cannot be said for cookbooks per se; one need only consult a library catalog to see the form is shifting rapidly.[1] Cookbooks are a genre worthy of study, with parameters and characteristics shared with other more self-consciously "literary" texts.[2] Susan J. Leonardi has observed that recipes are narratives in their own right, and that the texts in which they dwell merit our consideration.[3] Anne L. Bower further argues that in fact readers have long seen cookbooks as a literary genre, claiming that by reading cookbooks carefully we learn new ways of approaching traditional literary works, and of understanding the varieties of American life and culture.[4] Cookbooks and the recipes they contain present opportunities for authors to script a self, tell an exotic tale, recall a history, or, as I will argue here, mourn a lost loved one or memorialize a vanished place.

A classic of culinary literature with which Black chefs have contended, *The Alice B. Toklas Cookbook*, with its obvious ethnic stereotypes, throws into relief the ways in which writerly African American foodways simultaneously memorialize and promote Black culture. We need only recall Vertamae Smart-Grosvenor, whose acerbic retort that she not be seen as a "black Toklas" announced her rejection of that culinary forebear as well as her awareness of that ancestry, for their dissimilarity does not rule out all likeness. If there is no mention of African Americans or Africans in Toklas's memoir, its racialized subtext manifests the author's unwillingness to grant her talented "Asian" cooks agency and intelligence.[5] Toklas can be compared to the authors of the "mammy" cookbooks who patronizingly complimented the "untaught genius" of their African American cooks.

In contrast, recording traditional cookery and meals is a thoughtful way of measuring and commemorating a way of life, whether as an individual couple, a vanishing expatriate community, or an African American small town. Finally celebrated late in life, the chef and caterer Edna Lewis dedicated *The Taste of Country Cooking* (1976) "to the memory of the people of Freetown [Virginia]," an African American community of former slaves and their descendants.[6] *The Alice B. Toklas Cookbook* (1954), written by the expatriate American whose fame is inextricably linked to her longtime companion Gertrude Stein, ostensibly meditates on "the differences in eating habits and general attitude to food and the kitchen in the United States and [France]" ("A Word with the Cook," n.p.).[7] The books share certain structures and parallel events, but the correspondences both reflect and obscure each woman's ethnic identity or autobiographical elements. In her prefatory "A Word with the Cook," Toklas "confide[s] that this book with its mingling of recipe and reminiscence . . . was written as an escape from the narrow diet and monotony of illness [but also from] nostalgia for old days and old ways" (n.p.). Lewis begins by writing that the book grew out of living far away but longing for "the people I grew up with and our way of life" (xxi). As David E. Sutton has observed in his study of culinary recall, "Deprivation in the present creates . . . a space for the bubbling up of memories of hunger past, of another kind of history from below."[8] The introductions, and the presentation of their recipes, show how cookbooks function as methods of fixing memory as well as meal planning.[9] Some memories stem from a literal hunger, and others from an appetite for the past. Toklas looks back on a vanished life and mourns its passing; Lewis, often nostalgic in tone, sees that past life as a path to the future.

The two volumes can be seen as more than culinary compendia if we consider their deliberate engagement with loss.[10] If Virginia Woolf can remark that her novels might best be called elegies, so too can a collection of recipes.[11] But getting a meal on the table can also be viewed as a *sankofa*, a way of looking backward so that one can move forward. Sometimes figured as a bird with its head and feet facing in opposing directions, the Ghanaian sankofa, which symbolizes forward and backward motion, has become a metaphor for the necessity of Black Americans to reconnect with an African past.[12]

I use the word "sankofa" as others might use "elegy," another term that can describe works such as those of Lewis and Toklas: "a formal and sustained lament in verse for the death of a particular person, usually ending in a consolation."[13] Such lamentations can recall a vanished era or people, not solely an individual. Just as Toklas's *Cook Book* departs from the classic elegy by its author's avowed nonliterariness—"as if a cook-book had anything to do with writing" (280)—Lewis's *Taste of Country Cooking* also does not appear to lament the past. Elegy, however, may be more than iterations of loss as two recent scholars have recognized. Jahan Ramazani, writing of the tradition of African American elegy emblematized by the verse of Langston Hughes, argues that the poet wrote "elegies for public figures, relatives, friends, and poets rang[ing] from the private to the collective . . . and the 'vernacular' to the 'standard'". And non-elite elegies, Max Cavitch has argued, comprise "a genre crucial to the making of literary histories."[14] If we accept elegy as Cavitch's "highly adaptable discourse, not just for mourning the dead but for communicating and managing anxieties," we see how authors such as Toklas and Lewis participate in this tradition.[15] Cookbooks continue the cultural function of memorials, even if their users do not recognize them as such.[16]

It is worth noting that many of the earliest examples of elegy were written by men and addressed to men.[17] And until fairly recently, cookbooks seemed a genre largely aimed at women, if not also written by women. Celeste Schenck's suggestion that women's elegies offer an alternate mode of grieving, one that does not end but in some way continues, contributes another turn of perspective. Do cookbooks, when written by women, present a genre gendered?[18] Cookbooks such as those of Lewis and Toklas are, in Caren Kaplan's words, "out-law genres"—they are forms that "break most obvious rules of genre."[19] Commemorative excursions expanding our expectations of the elegy, they re-shape the genre's look and intent. Mourning can and does coexist with collections of recipes, wound within the written frames in which such recipes are embedded and occasionally within the recipes themselves. So Alice B. Toklas's cookbook and Edna Lewis's *Taste of Country Cooking* each invoke mourned and vanished pasts, within and around the frame of food preparation—but for different ends.

By using the term "sankofa" we can place Lewis's volume within an African diasporic context, seeing where and how Lewis departs from the commonly held conception of elegy. Her calm recollections and scaffold of remembered days present an honorific of a community. In contrast to Toklas's offerings, Lewis's vernacular recipes and reminiscences reanimate a formerly enslaved people. Lewis does not dwell on the dead as forever lost, for she recalls the de-parted as a prototypical African American community; doing so constitutes her sankofa, hailing the deceased while moving ahead.[20] Events such as Emancipation Day open houses operate as culinary memorial celebrations, as we see when Lewis recreates the menu of an Emancipation Day dinner (158). Annual events such as Race Day and revivals are recreated through remembered meals.

For Lewis and Toklas, lost moments and individuals are reimagined through dishes and ingredients now obscure. Tellingly, these two cooks juxtapose personal losses with recollections of the slaughtered animals that fed the departed. If the cycle of life includes death, then Toklas's "Murder in the Kitchen" should be seen as part of the process of recalling those who have passed on.[21] In the chapter in which Toklas learns how to get dinner on the table in the absence of hired cooks, her account of culinary violence brings to mind elegy and loss. Edna Lewis's description of hog-killing time also recounts a lost time and a lost community, via the remembered business of home butchery, a necessity for rural folk. If elegy and sankofa address death and loss, the cook's tales of once-living flesh and the meals they enabled illuminate modes of mourning or commemoration. If, as Carol Adams has said, "Animals are the absent referent in the act of meat eating" (14), the remembered act of butchering gestures to other absences.[22]

Because they approach loss differently, Toklas and Lewis take disparate approaches to the killing that accompanies omnivorous eating. The human predilection to eat anything and everything is one way individuals participate in death and belonging: to be a member of the community of omnivores, whether in Freetown, Virginia, or Paris, France, one must take part in a culinary system that calls for the killing of other animals. The recollection of the everyday violence entailed in cooking takes on nuance when incorporated into a culinary memoir: an animal's death makes real the loss that propelled the writing of the text, making literal the knowledge that something has passed. A living creature has been stilled, and a human community has dwindled from the actual to the historical. The twinned elements of mourning and memory add to both books a postlapsarian feel—that sense of loss for departed days.

Much of the daily life of Toklas and Gertrude Stein could be seen as bourgeois or upper middle class. They lived in a picturesque Paris flat and had a country home; they employed a cook; they collected art; they traveled widely. Yet Stein and Toklas, a lesbian couple, represented a lifestyle few Americans were then willing to publicly espouse. They were also nonpracticing Jews. Whatever their identities, Toklas does not emphasize the time she spent in the kitchen. References to Stein's writing career appear from time to time, but much of what Toklas records is luncheon and dinner excursions, punctuated by visits to and from notable creative and wealthy individuals: when Toklas and Stein attended "a lunch party . . . at a house whose mistress was a well-known French hostess and whose food was famous," they were served such delicacies as "Aspic de Foie Gras" and "Pheasants Roasted with Truffles . . . accompanied by appropriate and rare wines" (11).[23] Toklas aims to make American cooking French, not the other way around.

Toklas furthermore takes the American reader on an opinionated tour through classic French gastronomy.[24] Recipes for classics of the French table, such as "Boeuf Bourguignon" and "Quenelles," abound. Toklas does identify American contributions to culinary history as ingenious, and one could say her acknowledgment of the American zeal for convenience foods and pre-packaging paves the way for her later meditations on death and eating. Such bloodless options disconnect readers from meat eating and killing. Alluding to the separation between life and eating, Toklas writes that knowledge of pre-mealtime "sudden death[s] . . . doesn't apply to food that emerges stainless from deep freeze. But the marketing and cooking I know are French [rather than American]" (37). Eaters in France and the rural American South know where their rosbif comes from, and that eating a spring navarin necessitates the death of a sheep.

Toklas's "Murder in the Kitchen," meant to invoke the "crime and murder stories" Gertrude Stein so loved, engages the queasy connections between eating and death. She affirms that "facts, even distasteful facts, must be accepted . . . [and] before any story of cooking begins, crime is inevitable. That is why cooking is not an entirely agreeable pastime" (37). Her recollections of two wars and the occupation of France underscore this disagreeable subtext, for it is during wartime that Toklas must face a shortage of hired help and ingredients. She also must take on the role of executioner: "It was in those conditions of rationing and shortage that I learned not only to cook seriously but to buy food in a restricted market and not to take too much time doing it. . . . It was at this time, then, that murder in the kitchen began" (37). Toklas's "first victim" was "a lively carp brought to the kitchen in a covered basket from which nothing could escape" (37). Faced with the task of dispatching the fish by herself, Toklas reflects in mock hard-boiled fashion: "A heavy sharp knife came to my mind as the classic, the perfect choice. . . . The carp was dead, killed, assassinated, murdered in the first, second and third degree."

She then prepares and serves the fish, distancing the act of killing through parodic humor. Toklas's ambivalence about the killing must be made comic if they are to eat.

A basket of cooing doves brings closer the connection of meat eating and homicide. When Toklas returns to "Paris and then there was war and after a lifetime later there was peace," privations still exist. A friend from the country sends a half dozen doves, knowing that she "will make something delicious of them" (39). As Stein "didn't like to see work being done" (40), Toklas smothers the birds, in the way Jeanne, the cook, had taught her.[25] She finds, however, "one saw with one's fingertips as well as with one's eyes . . . a most unpleasant experience." Yet "as I laid out the sweet young corpses there was no denying one could become accustomed to murdering" (40). The dead birds make more powerful Stein's impending fatal illness, a loss that Toklas cannot explicitly articulate.[26] Other deaths go unrecorded, as Toklas does not differentiate between the general devastation of the Second World War and Hitler's specific genocidal campaign against the Jews.[27] Whether in the *Cook Book* or elsewhere, Toklas shrinks from direct engagement with undesirable realities and the unutterably sad: about the final time she saw Stein, when her lover was being wheeled into an operating room, Toklas laconically states, "and I never saw her again" (173).[28] Stein's death, like the Holocaust, takes place offstage.

To Edna Lewis, the slaughtering of an animal is not a subject for humor, but neither does it make an elliptical reference to human carnage. Published almost exactly twenty years after Toklas's *Cook Book*, Lewis's *The Taste of Country Cooking* is a cookbook with reminiscences. Lewis's memories are not simply an individual's story; they are one with the community. Her introductory sentence echoes the incantatory "I was born" of countless slave narratives, those autobiographies that present an individual as synecdochic with the group: "I grew up in Freetown, Virginia, a community of farming people. . . . The name was adopted because the first residents had all been freed from chattel slavery and they wanted to be known as a town of Free People" (xiii). Lewis writes her book because "I realize how much the bond that held us [her siblings] had to do with food. Since we are the last of the original families, with no children to remember and carry on, I decided that I wanted to write down just exactly how we did things when I was growing up" (xv). The vanished community could become a subject for elegy, a putting-aside of grief to laud those who have gone before.[29] One might accurately say that *The Taste of Country Cooking* is a series of praises in the form of linked memories and recipes.

Lewis does not recall meals with the famous and the royal. Her dishes limn a social milieu with a hierarchy that possesses parameters and norms of its own. Within the community, her grandparents—who helped build Free-town—were recognized as dynastic heads. Not "Bourbon kings," they were nonetheless a kind of royalty, as Lewis's grandfather had been "one of the first: His family, along with two others, were granted land by a plantation owner. . . . [In all, nearly a dozen families] built their houses in a circle around my grand-father's, which was in the center" (xiii). Lewis recalls midwinter with its near cessation of farming work as a time of visitors, although most came "to visit with Grandpa." She recalls how these elders would congregate, still awestruck by the transition from slavery to freedom. "There would be lively conversa-tions with the aged men doing most of the talking" (227). As one of the origi-nal settlers, Lewis's grandfather continued to exert a centrifugal power.

Before the quiet of a long winter settled in, the families of Freetown butch-ered hogs and preserved their flesh so that meat would be available all year long. Rather than displace a necessary action with humor, Lewis discusses the slaughter without metaphor, asserting that "hog killing was one of the spe-cial events of the year and generally took place in December . . . [for] a good three days of hanging in the open air" were necessary for the carcasses to be firm enough to cut up properly (181). While Lewis describes in detail the way the animals are prepared, she does not refer to events prior to that prepara-tion other than "each hog was killed." The dead animals are "beautiful . . . glis-tening white inside . . . and their skin was almost translucent" (182). No mov-ing, breathing animals appear, as in Toklas. These creatures are dispatched out of view, then brought on as "glistening . . . translucent" physical evidence of shared foodways. The slaughtering binds the Lewis family to the entire com-munity for its members help one another to prepare the winter's provisions. These deaths do not stand in for future losses but instead invoke together-ness; hog killing is acknowledged as a necessary prelude to meals. There is a feeling of joyousness and anticipation of the approaching holidays, for meals after a hog butchering provide an annual bounty: sweetbreads, lard, shoulders, bacon. Even the pigs' bladders were inflated, dried, and "made . . . part of our Christmas decorations" (182). Nothing that can be utilized gets discarded.

If hog butchering is presented as a yearly necessity, the selection of other animals for harvesting provokes ambivalence. When wild animals are maimed or destroyed in the course of plowing, Lewis points out that the babies would be saved: "if the [destroyed] quail turned out to be a hen, we [children] would hunt for her nest and, when we found the eggs, we'd set them under a bantam or give them to someone who had a hen. After they hatched, the quail chicks would stay [in the barnyard] . . . until they were big enough to return to the wild" (52). Lewis and her siblings would rescue "chickens, baby calves, pigs, and lambs that were too weak and unaggressive to compete for food. All such animals would be kept in the kitchen until the severe cold weather was over and they were strong enough." Although the children might have a favorite, even these saved critters would eventually be sold, leading to "a sad day for us"; the facts of life, Lewis says, "were explained to us as we grew up" (2). She admits that one "usually thinks of lamb as a spring dish but no one [in Lewis's family] had the heart to kill a lamb. The lambs were sold at the proper time and the sheep would be culled" (4). There were times for harvesting, both vege-table and animal, and Lewis's simultaneously matter-of-fact and affecting rec-ollections reflect the ambivalence inherent in raising animals to eat.

Nonetheless, Freetown takes center stage, not its domestic animals. The recipes that follow Lewis's reminiscences assist the reader to see a culinary sankofa, a backward look at those crisp late fall days and the people who popu-lated them. This format recurs throughout, with descriptions of specific events or seasons preceding a selection of recipes; sometimes the recipes are woven through the memories. Dishes such as black raspberries and cream, eggs from the family's own hens, fried sweetbreads from recently killed hogs, and apples browned in bacon fat jostle for space on her menus. Instructions for preparing an old-fashioned dish sometimes come in discursive rather than instructional format:

> The black raspberries were particularly good for preserving because they re-mained firm. . . . We would mix the berries with an equal amount of sugar and place them in glass bottles. Then we would cork the necks with a piece of cotton and pour melted wax over the tops. We would keep the filled bottles in an open-ing in the ground under a board in the kitchen floor and bring them out on spe-cial occasions like hog-butchering day because the flavor was so exotic. I have never forgotten the taste of them. (185)

If the remembered meals of Toklas revel in luxury, Lewis's Freetown meals re-call another kind of abundance—the sort that means one has enough to eat.

The dining table did not always display a bounty of fresh or sufficient in-gredients; seasonality and ingenuity shaped the meal. As foods come into sea-son Lewis celebrates them within a temporal menu: "An Early Spring Dinner" brings "Skillet Wild Asparagus" and "Salad of Tender Beet Tops, Lamb's-Quarters, and Purslane," among other fresh comestibles (8); in "A Snowy Winter Breakfast," "Oven-Cooked Ham Slices" and "Stewed Quinces" (230) portray the food preservation that pays dividends months later. The herbs Lewis encourages her readers to grow on city windowsills were in Virginia largely "uncultivated [growing] in the corners and along the sides of our garden: sage, horseradish, black basil, thyme, chervil, peppermint" (260). Whether clipped moments before use or dried to flavor future meals, the garden herbs that Toklas and Lewis employed would for some years vanish from the daily tables of most Americans. If for Toklas the disappearance of such garden luxuries was an occasion for mourning, for Lewis their absence spurred a call for revival.

An aging Toklas ended her book with their last harvest in the Rhone Valley. Although there is no talk of killing or kitchen murder in "The Vegetable Gardens at Bilignin," loss shades each paragraph. Toklas leads us through a veritable seed catalog of vegetables grown and harvested, plots tried out and abandoned, orchards started but failed. Raspberries and strawberries, string beans and beets, lettuces, corn, and squash—all are recalled affectionately. Once Toklas's vegetable beds have been harvested, their produce piled satisfyingly in baskets to take back to Paris, the "denuded wet cold garden [remains.] Our final, definite leaving . . . came one cold winter day, all too appropriate to our feelings and the state of the world. A sudden moment of sunshine peopled the gardens with all the friends and others who had passed through them . . . so we left Bilignin, never to return" (280).[30] Toklas does not say that they were trading their country home for an unknown future: in 1943, optimism could not stave off the reports of Nazi mass murders. Although she likely wrote "final definite leaving" (280) as a recapitulation of her last words with her lover, Toklas does not directly link the inability to return with Stein's death. In this way the Toklas cookbook serves as an elegy for a vanished way of life as well as for the deceased Stein. As she writes of earlier days of scarcity: "In the beginning, like camels, we lived on our past" (203). Toklas recounts "what is remembered," or rather what she would most like to have remembered—not what remained.

Compellingly, *The Taste of Country Cooking* does not end with a dark, denuded garden and sorrowing over vanished days of companionship and status. Lewis offers lessons from the past for the living. Her closing pages give us recipes for a cozy winter dinner with chicken and dumplings and warm gingerbread. Plangent feelings for bygone times appear in her introduction, which gestures to those "founders of Freetown [who] have passed away." Praise follows for the "many young people [who] are going back to the land and to the South. They are interested . . . in the past" (xv). Lewis recaptures a specific southern American—African American—space so that the next generation can carry it forward. She does not close on an elegiac note because her memories of childhood community mean to inspire a later generation to reinvent that long-ago place. In an interview some years later, Lewis affirmed that "as a child in Virginia, I thought all food tasted delicious. After growing up, I didn't think food tasted the same, so it has been my lifelong effort to try and recapture those good flavors of the past."[31] When Lewis uses the first or third person plural, asserting that "corn pone is legendary in our history" and invoking Paul Laurence Dunbar's poem on that food (21), or writing that "slavery lingered with us still" (117), she asks us to look behind so we can move into the future. She depicts guinea fowl, black-eyed peas, and sorghum of Freetown as ancestral culinary souvenirs, if I may pun on bringing back something to remember.[32] Lewis's family history and cultural past transform *The Taste of Country Cooking* into an elegy that goes beyond mourning and consolation to commemoration and a path forward.

Cookbooks and the recipes within reanimate departed loved ones and absent communities. Deaths too are recalled—the animals killed to feed a community, the individuals and peoples who pass on. They reappear in recipes that mourn and praise, as sankofa that point to a future shaped by the past. As scripted sites of memory cookbooks are often written by those who do not think of themselves as authors, but who deliver remarkable texts all the same. Toklas may have scoffed that a cookbook has nothing to do with writing, but recipes indeed have much to do with literary remembrance. As Lewis invites us to, let us muse on the "ideas [that] do live on for us to learn from, to enlarge upon, and pass on to the following generations . . . to share with everyone who may read this a time and a place that is so very dear" (xv). Then we too will forge the connection between meals of the past and today.

The Negro Cooks Up His Past

Arturo Schomburg's
Uncompleted Cookbook

Among the papers of the Puerto Rican–born Arturo (a.k.a. Arthur) Alfonso Schomburg, one of the twentieth century's most important bibliophiles, rests an unpublished manuscript labeled "[cookbook]."[1] Many scholars of the Schomburg Center for Research in Black Culture and its founder, and even his descendants, have little idea that the noted archivist of the African diaspora showed a serious interest in food.[2] Schomburg's typescript, including a page in his own hand, proposes a historical Black gastronomy divided "into three parts—Morning, Noon and Night—with appropriate meal time victuals and between-time snacks."[3] His plan, to make visible the "negro genius" in gastronomy, was in keeping with his life's work. The archetypical unsung individual who "adapted the English, French, Spanish and Colonial receipts taught him by his masters . . . to his own temperamental needs" would be celebrated along with "his own peculiar artistic powers" (1). So he would acknowledge the unsung talents of the many whose names went unrecorded.[4] As he so famously wrote in *The New Negro*, "The Negro has been a man without a history because he has been considered a man without a worthy culture."[5] Schomburg's projected gastronomy would script a master recipe for respect, a culinary narrative complementing the history and achievements of Black people.

That Schomburg's groundbreaking compendium was never completed is something of a mystery. Textual evidence dates its composition around 1930, suggesting there were some years between its initial draft and his death in 1938. Its unfinished state perhaps attests to the vastness of the subject he contemplated coupled with the scant primary sources available. Menus, cookbooks, and hospitality guides were even more rare than the "books, pamphlets, prints and old engravings . . . [writings on] social service and reform . . . [and] efforts towards race emancipation, colonization, and race betterment" that made up nearly the entire original collection.[6] If scholarship of the African diaspora was still in its early stages, even more nebulous would have been the study of Black domestic service, cookery, and foodways, a subject supported by rich anecdotal evidence but few documents.[7] Whatever his initial intentions, what remains of Schomburg's volume are fewer than two dozen pages of historical survey, a bit of personal memoir, an extensive list of recipe titles, a few handwritten notes, and a single recipe for okra gumbo taken from Lafcadio Hearn's classic New Orleans cookbook.[8]

Of the extant twenty-two manuscript pages, nine are arranged in menu format, broken down into daily mealtimes with subheads for categories such as breads and meats. The introductory pages indicate he planned to write biographies of prominent and little-known cooks alike and reveal the history of cooking in the United States as shaped by those of African descent. The handwritten notes (figure 7.1) that follow the typed proposal and precede the *La Cuisine Creole* recipe for "Gumbo of Okra or Filee" illustrate the range of Schomburg's inquiry. Schomburg's tome could have been an omnibus that stretched over centuries, American states, and extranational locales. The enormous scope was in keeping with Schomburg's collection, an unparalleled gathering of materials about those of African descent, housed under one roof. His gastronomy would showcase "the negro genius" in gastronomic history by discussing the recipes prepared by Blacks, presenting "personality sketches of many . . . famous Negro cooks—past and present," and celebrating the folk arts and lore that constitute vernacular cookery.

Schomburg's proposal asserted that cuisine prepared and developed by African Americans ranged from the simplest homestyle meal to elaborate, French-derived feasts. Within its pages are acknowledged the two streams of Black gastronomy dating from slavery times, noting "cabin cooking and cooking for the big house" while suggesting the Black diner's preference "for his own flavory [*sic*] dishes as contrasted with the more elaborate ones which he prepared in his masters' kitchens" (7).[9] The dishes included also tend to hail from foodways associated with the American South, a perception that still persists. Even as diets slowly changed in the nineteenth century, as slaves accessed more Europeanized foodstuffs and the forced migration of Africans to the southeastern United States declined, the "'African culinary grammar' survived."[10] The work of diasporic food scholars such as Jessica Harris, Leland Ferguson, and Judith Carney, who have written extensively about African gas-

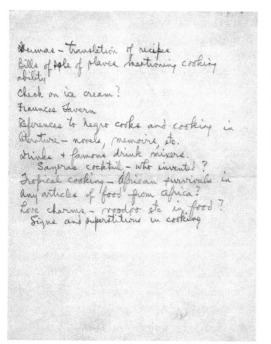

FIGURE 7.1 The sole handwritten page from the Schomburg "cookbook." Courtesy of the Schomburg Center for Research in Black Culture, Photographs & Prints Division.

tronomic legacies, lay decades in the future.[11] Schomburg's culinary history would have been the first to remark on key differences between "big house" and "quarters" dining, a distinction that can be seen across regions.

Schomburg emphasized certain elements in his scaffolding for a diaspora cuisine, as demonstrated by the inclusion of Hearn's "Gumbo of Okra or Filee" recipe and reproduced practically to the last comma. This sole complete recipe speaks—intentionally or not—to the metonymic status of an African diasporic cuisine. If we are what we eat, our foodstuffs similarly identify our culture. Thus gumbo, a vegetable whose name reflects either Bantu or Kikongo provenance, stands in for Black folks and southern cuisine as a whole. A mélange of ingredients from African, European, and Native American cuisines, gumbo is also associated closely with New Orleans and Louisiana. Made with "filee," the dish could exhibit a Native American layer, since filé powder is made from dried and pulverized sassafras leaves, favored as a thickener by indigenous Americans. (A note to the cook: this might not be considered a gumbo in the eponymous sense, as Hearn and most cooks today say gumbo should not use both filé and okra.) Yet certain items Schomburg includes, such as "buttermilk cakes" or "chitterlings," would be hard to identify as coming from a specific cultural group or region, whether the Crescent City or West Africa. The extensive range of dishes attests to how far Schomburg moved beyond Louisiana and Creole cuisine to craft a master narrative for a Black American gastronomy.

Schomburg was unable to settle on a single direction for his undertaking: would it be a culinary history, an encyclopedia of gastronomy, or a cookbook? Any approach would have been staggering considering the extent of the New World Black diaspora; in fact, what is extant does not encompass a truly global scope. While he proclaimed he would "discuss . . . various specialities from Haiti and the West Indies . . . uncover[ing] if possible such traces of Africanism which still persist in American dishes" (9), and despite his own upbringing in Puerto Rico and Saint Croix, Virgin Islands, Schomburg largely omits African-inflected cuisines of the Caribbean and South America. Items culled from outside of Francophone and Anglophone America are limited to "Brazilian" onions, Cuban-style hot chocolate, and "Xalapa" boudins. Only a few times does he remark on West Indian specialties or "tropical" markets under Harlem's elevated train, even though his biographer Vanessa Valdès has elsewhere noted his "diasporic blackness" and imbrication within the Puerto Rican and Cuban independence movements.[12] Outright references to the continent are nearly absent, one being "the delectable Fish Head Stew served to millionaire fisherman on Sea Island . . . similar [to a] concoction prepared by the Djuka negroes" of Surinam, Maroon descendants of escaped enslaved African peoples. Perhaps his focus on dishes found in the United States had to do with his teenaged self's migration to New York City, where he would marry more than one African American woman and raise his children, as well as the unfinished status of the work.

Viewed as autobiography, Schomburg's recall of "sugar-baked apples" and "ineffable steeped coffee" charms. One can almost hear Schomburg sighing happily as he writes of "batter cakes with borders of crisp black embroidery" or "cinnamon flavored chocolate and hot toddies." Many of these tasty offerings were served in "the home of my friend W. W. Cohen . . . a Negro and a Catholic—endowed with a Semitic name (1)."[13] A two-page list of morning recipes eventually follows, with subsections on "hot breads, griddle cakes and waffles," "breakfast meats," "other breakfast main dishes," "breakfast beverages," and "preserves." But first, rather than delving deeper into the breakfasts whipped up by Black cooks over the decades, or going on to survey other daily dishes, Schomburg pivots to the question that underpins his discussion: What makes the Black man a "genius" in the kitchen? Conceivably stimulated by his contemplation of the bounties of a lazy New Orleans breakfast among "sun streaked jalousies," Schomburg detours into a historical disquisition on Black chefs. The two whose renown began the lineage of African American celebrity chefs do not lead off his investigation.

Before twentieth-century New Orleans breakfast rooms, only a handful of Black cooks could be identified by first name, much less surname. James Hemings, chef to Thomas Jefferson, and the even earlier reigning Hercules, known as the runaway chef of George Washington, today head the list of historical African American chefs, but Schomburg should not be criticized for omitting them. Unlike Robert Roberts and Tunis Campbell, they left behind no volumes of their own; only tangentially through histories of Washington and Jefferson do we learn about the chefs they enslaved.[14] Schomburg could and did write about one colonial and early national-era figure, Samuel "Black Sam" Fraunces of New York City's Fraunces Tavern fame, whose personal connection to Washington had been amply documented. Debates raged into the twentieth century over Fraunces's racial ancestry. While the innkeeper was once described as mulatto, any allegation of African identity was erased by historical societies invested in the tavern's preservation, notably by the Daughters of the American Revolution and Sons of the Revolution in the State of New York.[15] In one of his published articles Schomburg referred to "the enigma of the man. . . . Few knew [his] racial background," while at the same time pointing out that an early nineteenth-century portrait depicted Fraunces as "a mulatto."[16] Fraunces may have fascinated Schomburg in part because of the scarcity of data about early Black cookery. We already know few African American chefs left recorded testimony; extant published works were rare. That those elusive figures went without mention is understandable, even before taking into account the unfinished nature of the project. A better unanswered question might be, what published cookbooks and works of culinary history were acquired before the curator's death in 1938?[17] If Schomburg had not read the cookbooks of Roberts, Fisher, and their peers, how could he begin?

Schomburg praised Black culinary artists known to him, whether Dan (or Bill) Singleton or Mrs. Mordecai Johnson.[18] Remarks in the manuscript indicate he knew others. George Washington Carver could well have been the source for "fried pies—especially delicious when made with wild plums," as the celebrated botanist was certainly known to Schomburg and might even have been an acquaintance.[19] William Crum, said to have invented the potato chip in a Saratoga restaurant—to be included under "Irish potato recipes" (17)—almost certainly never met Schomburg, although his fame reached to the city of New York and possibly to the bibliophile's circle.[20] Historically Black institutions other than Carver's Tuskegee offered culinary and nutritional science curricula, so Hampton Institute's Carrie Alberta Lyford's book "for the Cooking School" might well have provided some of the directions for mealtime staples.[21] While we can never ascertain definitively which recipes Schomburg collected from working chefs, we can locate some of the published sources of his Black culinary masterpieces. If his encyclopedia was to "rescue from oblivion . . . these unknown artists," to begin the recovery Schomburg would have to start with the results of their work: the extant published recipes. Ironically, white homages to the Black cook's art provided a resource.

Patronizingly titled compilations such as *Mirations and Miracles of Mandy* and *Mammy Lou's Cookbook* give away the biases of their authors.[22] These books would laud the skills of the African American female cook while asserting her childishness, illiteracy, and opacity, as did so many others.[23] As their recipes reveal African American culinary expertise, the books undercut that knowledge. Schomburg had to reconcile the information found in texts celebrating the Old South with an Afrodiasporic gastronomy that honored its creators. By combing the records of what was available and including the specific creations of Black chefs, Schomburg reverse engineered an African diasporic culinary culture.

The career of William Deas, whose name was linked to several recipes collected by Schomburg, demonstrates the bibliophile's tactics of using nostalgia-laden cookbooks to reclaim an honored past. "Shrimpsoup—William Deas' recipe" illustrates Schomburg's methodology. Keywords entered into an internet search engine—"Negro cook," "shrimp soup," and "William Deas"—delivered several hits, the "bingo" being the blog of South Carolina chef Forrest Parker. Beyond providing "the lost recipe of William Deas," Parker cited the cookbook that had first celebrated Deas's skills: Blanche S. Rhett's *Two Hundred Years of Charleston Cooking*, published in 1930.[24] Deas, "one of the greatest cooks in the world" (2), worked as the butler for Charleston mayor Goodwyn Rhett—the husband of the cookbook's author. In the introduction Helen Woodard wrote, "What you eat in Charleston today is a slowly ripened mixture of French and Negro cooking" (x). Whether or not Deas and Schomburg ever met, the two men were active during the same era, so the possibility is there. However Schomburg learned about *Two Hundred Years*, he believed that its recipes provided a window into African American culinary artistry. "William's veal and chesnutt stuffing" (16) and others of his creations appear in both the published volume and Schomburg's manuscript, confirming the decision to recover Black talent from problematic sources.[25]

Schomburg's difficult choice, to recreate a culinary history via the publications of those who would suppress that history, can be seen in Rhett's referencing of two Black men who made their livings through food. Deas, the chef employed by the Rhetts, is regularly cited, although he is nowhere depicted in the book. Instead, the book provides a photograph of an unnamed individual, a Charleston "potato farmer," dressed in ragged work clothing, balancing a sack of his produce atop his head (figure 7.2). The images reproduced in this chapter mark the genteel racism that on the one hand can acknowledge the professionalism of an employee while at the same time undercut that skilled worker by the inclusion of an anonymous, "folkloric" image. Taken later in life, the portrait included here of Deas (figure 7.3), in spotless professional gear at the Charleston restaurant Everett's, underscores his pride and accomplishment: as the son of the late Everett Preston attested, "He was a very refined gentle soul with impeccable manners."[26]

The Blue Grass Cook Book by Minnie C. Fox, another nostalgic compilation of southern cookery, is also worth exploring to uncover Schomburg's approach. While Fox's pictures may differ from Rhett's, *Blue Grass's* modern editor, Toni Tipton-Martin, avers, "The written word has been cruel to African American cooks."[27] With an introduction by the author's brother John Fox and illustrations by photographer A. L. Coburn, *Blue Grass's* individual recipes are usually credited to whites who are listed in a roll call of contributors (xlvii–xlviii); the book is specifically dedicated to four white women. Early on the mythic Black female cook appears, rhapsodized by John Fox as the "turbaned mistress of the Blue Grass kitchen . . . broad, portly, kind of heart" (xxxvi). Unlike in *Two Hundred Years*, the creations of the women in *Blue Grass* are nearly all uncredited, save for a recipe for "Nan's candy" (345). Of the eight captions under photographs of women, only two identify the subjects by name.[28] Unexpectedly, then, while the "turbaned mistresses" devolve into a stereotype, a Black man is repeatedly recognized for his individual contributions.[29] Cap-

FIGURE 7.2 Photograph of potato
farmer from *Two Hundred Years of
Charleston Cooking.* Courtesy Cornell
University Libraries.

tured smiling into the camera, Marcellus (figure 7.4) is professionally attired
with a long apron protecting his pants, a dark vest over his white shirt, and a
tie (172).[30] The William Deas of *Blue Grass* country, Marcellus is credited with
no fewer than seven recipes, including two for ice creams. In contrast to the
Rhett volume, Marcellus's documented expertise resulted in the inclusion of a
respectful photograph along with his recipes. Nonetheless, although acknowledged as a valuable employee, Marcellus does not receive the respect inherent
in the giving of a surname.

FIGURE 7.3 William Deas in toque, at Everett's in Charleston. Courtesy of Everett Presson.

With little to go on beyond the recipes in white-authored, nostalgia-driven volumes, Schomburg still intended to write the biographies and histories of renowned cooks, chefs, and restaurateurs. Ideally, the reader would find "personality sketches of . . . famous Negro cooks—past and present—and many of their best receipts—a great many of which have never been published" (3). Admitting that much of what we long to know is irrecoverable, Schomburg mused that "the well-known colored cooks are exceptional. . . . The true creative impulse in cooking as in all folk arts, is vested in anonymous thousands" (3). While "Nancy of Monticello" may be known only by her given name and the dish she presented to a visiting Lafayette (3), others known to Schomburg could share recipes.[31] Bill Singleton, the chef of Long Island's Stage Coach Inn, would reveal his "prized and private—Plantation chicken [recipe]—for thirty—a noble dish of boned fillets of chicken dipped in a special batter and fried softly—then served on a silver salver carried in by two waiters" (4).[32] Baltimore caterers Charles Shipley and Bernard Smith, mentioned in the extant text, might have been celebrated in the finished work along with others from "various cities of the North and South" such as Pig Foot Mary, one of Harlem's most famous entrepreneurs, and the "oyster man, the crab man, [and] the shrimp man" of the coastal South. Schomburg was well aware of the artistry and culinary entrepreneurship of these unnamed "anonymous thousands" who deeply enriched a South renowned for its abundance and gastronomy.

FIGURE 7.4 Marcellus, as he appears in *The Blue Grass Cook Book* by Minnie C. Fox. Courtesy of Michigan State Libraries.

Black culinary history perhaps proved so immense that the author may have realized that his finite time and resources would not do justice to the subject.[33]

For beyond amassing recipes and recording the biographies of chefs, Schomburg longed to reveal "how signs and seasonings sit side by side in the unwritten Negro cook book—how [for example] it is well known that an aged fowl is made tender by an iron nail" or that some dishes must be stirred in one direction while others call for stirring in the opposite (6). Such culinary commandments likely came from the Black folkways that Schomburg collected, which would also have included directions for the manufacture of aged and cured hams (5) and "lye hominy" (6). Notations for "drinks & famous drink mixers," "love charms," "voodoo," and "signs and superstitions in cookery" (n.p.) stand out in Schomburg's manuscript as provocative and suggestive advertisements for the narrative he envisioned. When one considers that he

FIGURE 7.5 Arturo Schomburg enjoying dinner with the painter William Scott and friends. Courtesy of the Schomburg Center for Research in Black Culture, Photographs & Prints Division.

hoped to add "receipts adapted to modern conditions" and time savers such as "a shrimp jambalaya which can easily be prepared in fifteen minutes" (11), the never-ending, ever-expanding scope of Schomburg's project becomes clear. Perhaps his was an impossible if delicious dream, but it is one that shows the grand scale of a Black cuisine.

Whether Schomburg specifically sought to obtain early cookbooks or hospitality books by Black authors may never be known.[34] Despite the lack of a physical trail for the research, Schomburg's culinaria exhibits fondness for the subject as well as an understanding of its importance. References to "homely delicac[ies]" and "delicious stuffed West Indian style crabmeat" (4, 11) reveal his love of dining well. His ceaseless travels on behalf of the Prince Hall Masons and his scholarly activities and collecting would have necessitated taking meals outside of his home, giving him frequent opportunity to sample regional cuisines with friends and acquaintances from New Orleans to Washington, D.C.[35] On the road, his meals must regularly have been taken with fellow Masons, colleagues and friends, or at private catered affairs, for without local insiders Schomburg would have had to find his meals in segregated establishments. Toward the end of his life, he might have even used *The Green Guide*, aide to the traveler of color before segregation barriers (mostly) fell.[36] Even in his beloved Harlem, restaurants were generally straightforward affairs aimed at feeding their clientele rather than showcasing the cook's culinary expertise. "The non-existence of any first-class Negro restaurant in Harlem" and "social and economic factors," Schomburg said, made "colored people . . . home eaters" (10). Beyond the precincts of the New Negro, upper-echelon New York City restaurants were off limits to most visibly nonwhite customers.[37] And although tourist venues of 1920s Harlem were known to attract whites, Schomburg scoffs at the voyeurs from downtown who believe they are getting the real thing, as in one such establishment's "leathery" fried chicken.[38]

Schomburg's "cookbook" may only have been an afternoon's musing for the busy bibliophile. Whatever his initial impetus and the unfinished state of his accomplishment, Schomburg offers more than a plan for a culinary history—among other things, we see an underappreciated and little-known memoirist of the New Negro. We learn about food and, tantalizingly, a bit about the life of a Black intellectual circa the 1930s. Like the personal missives he addressed to friends and colleagues, Schomburg's gastronomic excursion reveals a knowledgeable and opinionated personality who combined a love of dining with the lifelong pursuit of an accurate historical record. Read with the volumes by Black chefs beginning nearly two centuries ago, and complemented by the restored history of the little-known cooks who shaped our shared cuisine, Schomburg's text show us how much we still have to retrieve. Schomburg famously instructed "the Negro to dig up his past." His promised culinaria presents a menu to reclaim what must be remembered, whether as culinary memoir, sankofa, or recipe for respect.

Acknowledgments

For whatever reasons, authors tend to leave expressions of love and gratitude to their partners to the end—not me. So my dearest ones come first. William Paul attended to my years of complaining, mind-changing, and what-have-yous; thank you for your love and support. Thank you, Nathan, our son, for becoming a vegetarian to remind me that there are other ways to think about eating. Thank you to my sister, Maryam, who resolved to avoid the convenience foods beloved by our late mother and led the way to my acquiring kitchen skills. I wish my grandmother, Lethia Walker, could read this book: the years spent in her Harlem kitchen, being allowed to cut out baking powder biscuits or shake the chicken pieces for frying in a flour-filled brown paper bag, shaped me in ways I only in late adulthood began to understand.

The editors and readers of *Groupe Recherche Anglo-Américaine de Tours*, especially my friend and colleague Claudine Raynaud, provided me with encouragement and critical feedback; Sandra Gunning, Irma McClaurin, the four anonymous readers for *Feminist Studies*, and Doris Witt saw "The Signifying Dish" to its debut in the United States. Early encouragement came from Janice Longone and the Culinary Historian Societies of Ann Arbor, Michigan, and Cambridge, Massachusetts; the late John Egerton; and Shelley Fisher Fishkin and Jeff Meikle.

Two sponsoring entities offered me a critical year's leave: the National Endowment for the Humanities and the Schomburg Center for Research in Black Culture at the New York Public Library. Without their financial and academic support, I would not be writing these acknowledgements. My home institution, Washington University in Saint Louis, made sure the sabbatical happened.

Friends and colleagues in food studies cheered me on and cheered me up. More importantly, they provided me with a wealth of scholarship, intellectual sounding boards, and role models. Warren Belasco befriended me while I was a novice food studies scholar; his generosity and friendship are well known. Doris Witt's study confirmed the direction of my subject, and her hospitality underscored her genuine collegiality. Psyche Williams-Forson has seen this whole manuscript through and was unflagging in her encouragement. Anne Bower and Carole Counihan boosted me at the beginning. Kyla Wazana Tompkins and her work helped me restart. The Food, Culture, and Society community as a whole has been great, including Amy Bentley, Alice Julier, and Krishnendu Ray and virtually anyone else therein. Professor Kimberly Jackson and the faculty participants at the Spelman-Mellon colloquium on food allowed me to share some ideas. South Carolinians Forrest Parker and Everett Presson shared photographs and memories of William Deas. Saint Louis food studies colleagues Corinna Treitel and Glenn Stone love to talk shop. Two departed scholars in the field deserve recognition: Doris L. King, who published a modern edition of Tunis Campbell's guide, and "D. L. Frienze," the real-life Dianna Seay. Julie Dash and Rachel Watanabe-Bratton gave me the opportunity to talk on camera about Vertamae Smart-Grosvenor, whom sadly I never met.

The Schomburg Center offered a bounteous intellectual cadre: fellow scholars-in-residence Myra Armstead, John Perpener, Jim Smethurst, Jess Krug, Devyn Benson, Rashad Shabazz, Paula Austin, and Kristin Moriah were the best sounding boards a scholar could wish for; Farah Jasmine Griffin, scholar extraordinaire, along with Schomburg Fellows seminar leader historian Khalil Gibran Muhammad, then director of the Schomburg, rounded out a constellation of scholars. The Schomburg staff—starting with Maira Liriano and continuing with Stephen Fullwood, Shola Lynch, Diana Lachantere, Mary Yearwood, Miss Aisha, and my research assistant Melay Araya—tried to answer all of my questions. Many others at the Schomburg, whose names I am unable to recall should know I am grateful, if forgetful. Members of the Schomburg family inspired me.

Nearly twenty years ago the American Antiquarian Society awarded me a Peterson fellowship to work on nineteenth-century materials, giving me another crop of scholar friends: John Hench, Gigi Barnhill, Paul Erickson, Carolyn Sloat, Graham Hodges, and the Society's truly remarkable librarians. Additional props go to Graham Hodges for his work on Black entrepreneurship. And although I never made it to Tuskegee University's archives, I am grateful for Dana Chandler's assistance.

To Carla Peterson and Gabrielle Foreman: three cheers for the decades club. Shelley Fisher Fishkin, John Lowe, Elizabeth Higginbotham and Carla Kaplan: true friends all. Lynn Weiss and Werner Sollors: I know you remember when Nathan Huggins told me that this should be a "second book, your second book"; you hung in to see it happen. Nellie Y. McKay, Robin W. Kilson, Sacvan Bercovitch, and Nathan Austern: I miss you still.

My former colleagues at Michigan's Center for African and African American Studies well earned their shout-out: Earl Lewis, Robin D. G. Kelley, Michael Awkward, Elsa Barkley Brown, Neil Foley, Huma Ibrahim, and Sharon Patton. Ann Arborigines Avery Demond, Valerie Kivelson, Lisa C. Young, and Sharla Fett remain dear friends.

My colleagues at Washington University in Saint Louis, be they in African and African American Studies, English, or Olin Library, earn my esteem daily. Gerald Early brought me to Washington University and has edited me besides. I have further benefited from the lively crew in McMillan: Shanti Parikh, Sowandé Mustakeem, Tim Parsons, Mungai Mutonya, Wilmetta Toliver-Diallo, Jonathan Fenderson, Monique Bedasse, Jean Allman, Jeffrey McCune, Rebecca Wanzo, Carol Camp Yeakey, Iver Bernstein, Garrett Duncan, Bill Maxwell, Vetta Thompson, Samba Diallo, Ron Himes, Bill Tate, and John Baugh. Janary Stanton almost always let me barge into her office and before her, so did Adele Tuchler and Raye Mahaney. Duncker colleagues Guinn Batten, Jessica Rosenfeld, Dillon Brown, Melanie Micir, Vivian Pollak, Miriam Bailin, David Lawton, Wolfram Schmidgen, Carl Phillips, Mary Jo Bang, and so many more across the university have my gratitude. Administrators Meredith Lane, Sarah Hennessey, and Kari Alca kept me on the straight and narrow. Angela Miller has been my American Studies rock in Saint Louis—and someone whose cooking I am always ready to eat. Kimberly Norwood remains my friend and inspiration, from that first time years ago when we talked about the lack of New York City foods here. Adrienne Davis has not only been a model but also a crucial check on my procrastination. Jo Ellen Lewis egged me on to the finish. Joan Strassmann and David Queller taught me the mysteries of fermentation. WUSTL librarians—the steadfast Rudolph Clay, and colleagues past and present such as Makiba Foster, Cheryl Holland, Kristine Helbling, and Virginia Toliver—were always there, as were the Digital Humanities group, including Joe Loewenstein, Doug Knox, Stephen Pentecost, and Anupam Basu. Mary Laurita and the Mellon Mays Undergraduate Fellows at Washington University did more for me than they realize, as did graduate advisees from Crystal Alberts to Meredith Kelling.

Joycelyn Moody's friendship and scholarly wisdom remain a treasure. Lewis and Elisabeth Perry provided nearly two decades of dinners and great conversation, not to mention tomatoes and fish peppers. My Fulbright at Utrecht University in the Netherlands brought the friendship and good cheer of Derek Rubin, Jaap Verheul, Joke Kardux, and Edouard van de Bilt. My Ford Fellows family, from Yvette to Keivan to Koritha to Susan A. to Chris O'Brien and so many more it would take me all day and then some to name them: you keep me in the game. Laura Helton welcomed me into the unofficial Arturo Alfonso Schomburg society. Southern Foodways Alliance editors John T. Edge and Psyche Williams-Forson earned a heap of praise. Feedback givers from all over get my thanks: anonymous readers for the University of Georgia and MELUS; Lynn Weiss, Guinn Batten, and Jahan Ramazani considered passages on modernism. David Shields and Dana Nelson offered generous comments on early versions, as did book editors T. Susan Chang and Jennifer Crewe. Gerald Early, Amy Bentley, Martha Cutter, Anne Bower, Darra Goldstein, Gordon Hutner, and still others helped better this project over many years. Kiara Sample helped index. Emily Shelton stepped in at a crucial moment to review the entire manuscript; James Patrick Allen, copyeditor Lori Rider, and Rebecca Norton got things underway. Whatever omissions remain are mine.

Deborah Parks, Bruce Bacon, Jean Chase, Linda Tsai, Kumar Rao, Russ van Gelder, and Patty Croughan kept me going—they know why and how.

Friends from since who-knows-when may not realize how much they contributed, but their fingerprints are here. Marilyn Nance's public needling of me as being insufficiently revolutionary years ago on a Bronx corner surely had something to do with my ending up in African American studies. Roshanna Rothberg and Asif Rahman provided households in Hoboken and Elkview where I could ruminate and cook, not to mention admire their unflappable spirit. Arlene Zeichner long ago told me always to cook the recipe as written the first time around, and I almost always do. David and Karen Waltuck, friends since teenaged days of discovering Perrier and eating cassoulet stashed on New York City fire escapes—here we still are. Claudia Brown, Grace Wang, Danny Fingeroth, Richie Kahn, Evander Lomke, and others from my hometown dine out with me still. Old friends are gold friends.

And once again because he deserves thanks at the beginning and the end: this is for Bill.

Notes

INTRODUCTION. Food as a Field of (Black) Action

1. The phrase is from Mary Douglas, "Standard Social Uses of Food: Introduction," in *Food in the Social Order: Studies of Food and Festivities in Three American Communities*, ed. Mary Douglas (New York: Russell Sage Foundation, 1984), 30.

2. Toni Morrison, *Playing in the Dark* (New York: Vintage, 1993). I find her discussion of the shadow relevant; see 46–47.

3. James Weldon Johnson invoked the "gone, forgot, unfamed" writers of the spirituals, summoning to mind those long dead cooks whose names we will never learn. See Johnson, "O Black and Unknown Bards," in *The Book of American Negro Poetry* (1922; reprint, New York: Harvest/Harcourt Brace, 1969), 123–24.

4. *Sankofa*, an Akan word generally translated as "going back to move forward," has been adopted by many African Americans to refer to the necessity of knowing from whence one came. See my extended discussion in chapter 6.

5. Edna Lewis, "What Is Southern?" *Grantmakers in the Arts Reader: Ideas and Information on Arts and Culture* 19, no. 3 (Fall 2008): 3–4. Originally published in *Gourmet Magazine*, January 2008.

6. Michael Twitty, The Cooking Gene: A Journey through African American Culinary History in the Old South (New York: Amistad, 2017), xi–xii.

CHAPTER 1. Recipes for Respect

Portions of this chapter have previously appeared in *African American Foodways*, edited by Anne Bower (2007).

1. [Eliza Potter], *A Hair-Dresser's Experience in High Life* (1859; reprint, New York: Oxford University Press, 1988), iv.

2. After reading an early version of this work, Susan Strasser suggested that the phrase "home economists," which I used in an earlier draft, was anachronistic to this discussion; nevertheless, the phrase, with its connotation of "managing" the domes-

tic, would also serve to describe the labor that Campbell, Fisher, and Roberts perform. Strasser, personal communication, November 1997.

3. This is a multiple pun, the provenance of which must be attributed to P. Gabrielle Foreman. See Foreman's essay "Manifest in Signs: The Politics of Sex and Representation in *Incidents in the Life of a Slave Girl*," in *Harriet Jacobs and* Incidents in the Life of a Slave Girl: *New Critical Essays*, ed. Deborah Garfield and Rafia Zafar (Cambridge: Cambridge University Press, 1996), 76–99, as well as Karen Halttunen's *Confidence Men and Painted Women: A Study of Middle-Class Culture in America, 1830–1870* (New Haven, CT: Yale University Press, 1982), and "Dressing Up and Dressing Down" in Rafia Zafar's *We Wear the Mask: African Americans Write American Literature, 1760–1870* (New York: Columbia University Press, 1997), 151–84.

4. James Oliver Horton and Lois E. Horton, *Black Bostonians* (New York: Holmes & Meier, 1999), 25; James Oliver Horton and Lois E. Horton, *In Hope of Liberty* (Oxford: Oxford University Press, 1998), 239.

5. Roberts quoted in Horton and Horton, *Black Bostonians*, 91.

6. Cornish's diatribes against colonizationists are well known to readers of early Black periodicals. Issues of Cornish's *Rights of Man* and *Colored American* attest to the strength of native-born Blacks' considerable opposition to the removal of free Blacks to Africa. For examples, see https://www.wisconsinhistory.org/Records/Article/CS4415.

7. Hodges, introduction to Roberts, *The House Servants Directory: or, A Monitor for Private Families Comprising Hints on the Arrangement and Performance of Servants' Work* (Armonk, NY: M. E. Sharpe, 1998), xxxvi. Further references to this edition of Roberts will be given parenthetically within the text.

8. This American habit of asserting a typological link with God's chosen people goes back to the seventeenth century and English-born Puritans. Eighteenth-century Black Christian authors, whether the evangelical preacher John Marrant or the poet Phillis Wheatley, seized on the rhetoric of a chosen people as a means of both understanding their own, contemporary oppression and making their African identity more explicable and less threatening to their white counterparts in the United States. For one discussion of this rhetoric, see John Saillant, "'Remarkably Emancipated from Bondage, Slavery, and Death': An African American Retelling of the Puritan Captivity Narrative, 1820," *Early American Literature* 29, no. 2 (1996): 122–40.

9. For convenience I here take my definitions of "credit" from *The American Heritage Dictionary*, 2nd college edition (New York: Houghton Mifflin, 1991).

10. For a window into the political world of Robert Roberts and Tunis Campbell, see the Colored Conventions Project, http://coloredconventions.org/.

11. The phrase "somewhat more independent" is from Shane White's study, *Somewhat More Independent: The End of Slavery in New York City, 1770–1810* (Athens: University of Georgia Press, 1991). See also William Piersen, *Black Yankees: The Development of an Afro-American Subculture in Eighteenth-Century New England* (Amherst: University of Massachusetts Press, 1988), 46.

12. Tunis G. Campbell, *Hotel Keepers, Head Waiters, and Housekeepers' Guide* (Boston: Coolidge & Wiley, 1848). References to the *Guide* will be given parenthetically within the text. This text is available online at https://digital.lib.msu.edu /projects/cookbooks/html/books/book_17.cfm.

13. In contrast to Robert Roberts, Tunis Campbell published an autobiography: *Sufferings of the Rev. T. G. Campbell and His Family* (Georgia, WA: Enterprise, 1877). On his political life, see Russell Duncan's study *Freedom's Shore: Tunis Campbell and the Georgia Freedmen* (Athens: University of Georgia Press, 1986).

14. Campbell, *Sufferings*, 5. A small booklet of fewer than thirty pages, *Sufferings* devotes not even two pages to Campbell's pre–Civil War life (5–6).

15. Doris King, historian of American hospitality and editor of the first modern reprint of Campbell's guide, describes this nineteenth-century hotel practice: "Forced to feed dozens, sometimes hundreds, of people within an hour or two . . . some of [the hotelkeepers] adopted a military-style dining room 'drill' by which waiters, usually a corps of free black men or Irish immigrants, were trained to serve ordinary meals [that is, meals served in an '"ordinary'" or public house] quickly, efficiently, and in perfect time and step. The keepers, or their headwaiters, used voice commands, bells, or music as signals for the various movements." King republished Campbell's text as *"Never Let People Be Kept Waiting": A Textbook on Hotel Management* (Raleigh, NC: King Reprints in Hospitality Management, 1973), xii–xiii. Russell Duncan briefly draws the connection between Campbell's success as a politician and his early work in hotelkeeping; he doesn't specifically address the *Guide*, however. See *Freedom's Shore*, 15.

16. See Simon Gikandi, *Slavery and the Culture of Taste* (Princeton, NJ: Princeton University Press, 2011), 241.

17. By this I mean to suggest an instance of tactics, in the de Certeauian sense: serving could easily be viewed as a game played in another's territory and seemingly on another's terms, but working in consonance with the disadvantaged or weaker player's aims and goals. See Michel de Certeau, *The Practice of Everyday Life*, trans. Stephen Rendell (Berkeley: University of California Press, 1984), xviii–xx.

18. Many European travelers in early nineteenth-century America addressed the young nation's lack of civility and polish. See Alexis de Tocqueville, "Some Reflections on American Manners," in *Democracy in America* (1831), http://xroads.virginia .edu/~hyper/detoc/ch3_14.htm, and Frances Trollope, *Domestic Manners of the Americans* (1832), in which she asserted a "universal deficiency in good manners" among Americans. xroads.virginia.edu/~hyper/DETOC/FEM/trollope.htm.

19. Danya Pilgrim's study of the role of Black men in service in the city of Philadelphia similarly finds how working as waiters for whites supported the latter's desire for elevated social status; as a result of their expertise, Black men leveraged their own status from waiter to caterer. See Pilgrim, "Transforming Public Space: Black Men and Philadelphia Eating Culture," unpublished manuscript, May 2017.

20. Sterling Stuckey has argued that "slave dance in New England was not substantially different from black dance in the South," asserting "the presence in New England and the South of an African aesthetic of standard of beauty radically different from that of whites." *Slave Culture: Nationalist Theory and the Foundations of Black America* (Oxford: Oxford University Press, 1987), 77.

21. See the West Jersey History Project, http://www.westjerseyhistory.org/docs/gloucesterrecs/slavery/introandhelps.shtml. Later in adulthood Campbell would meet significant numbers of enslaved and/or African-born Americans as an elected official in Reconstruction-era Georgia.

22. Although Campbell didn't invent the drill, Doris King believes Campbell greatly improved on it, explaining the practice better than any of his contemporaries; see King, *Textbook on Hotel Management*, xiv.

23. In his research Shane White quotes Silvia DuBois, former slave from New Jersey, who remembers the Black militias of "Training Day." White, "'It Was a Proud Day': African-Americans, Festivals, and Parades in the North, 1741–1834," *Journal of American History* 81, no. 1 (June 1994): 13–50.

24. See the excellent scholarship on these processions by Geneviève Fabre, Shane White, and Sterling Stuckey, among others.

25. See Joseph Roach, *Cities of the Dead: Circum-Atlantic Performance* (New York: Columbia University Press, 1996), 9–11 and throughout, for an influential discussion of the ways a variety of physically enacted activities from different global locales reappear in the New World. I have discussed Campbell's moves relative to performance in an unpublished Modern Languages Association essay (2016).

26. Gikandi, *Slavery*, 235. Campbell's illustrations for what he calls a "serving drill" might reflect extant examples of Black exhortative typography such as David Walker's *Appeal* (1829) with which, as an educated abolitionist, he would have been familiar. See also Marcy J. Dinius's discussion of early Black print culture, "'Look!! Look!! At This!!!! The Radical Typography of David Walker," *PMLA* 126, no. 1 (January 2011): 55–72.

27. See Duncan, *Freedom's Shore*, and King, *Textbook on Hotel Management*, xxvii. King relies there on an account of Black legislators published in 1968.

28. Here I am very grateful to the late Dianna Seay, writing as D. J. Frienz, for biographical information on Bullock contained in her reprint of Bullock's volume, *173 Pre-Prohibition Cocktails: Potations So Good They Scandalized a President* (Jenks, OK: Howling at the Moon Press, 2001). See also Robert Simonson, "Tom Bullock's 'The Ideal Bartender' Offers Words of Advice," http://www.nytimes.com/2015/02/18/dining/tom-bullock-the-ideal-bartender-offers-words-of-advice.html?login=email&_r=0. Chantal Martineau quotes Bullock's grandnephew, who regrets not learning more about *The Ideal Bartender*'s author while his older relatives were still living. See Martineau, "Tom Bullock and the Forgotten Legacy of African American Bartenders," http://punchdrink.com/articles/tom-bollock-and-the-forgotten-legacy-of-african-american-bartenders/.

29. Thomas Bullock Jr., *The Ideal Bartender* (Saint Louis: Buxton & Skinner, 1917), 3. See also http://digital.lib.msu.edu/projects/cookbooks/books/idealbartender/bart .pdf.

30. Bullock, Ideal *Bartender*, 43. Bullock's famed skills likely reached Arturo Schomburg, who refers to a Pendennis julep in his cookbook; see chapter 7, "The Negro Cooks Up His Past," in this volume.

31. Earl Lewis, introduction to *In Their Own Interests: Race, Class, and Power in Twentieth-Century Norfolk, Virginia* (Chapel Hill: University of North Carolina Press, 1991), 1–7.

32. Susan J. Leonardi's essay on "Recipes for Reading: Summer Pasta, Lobster à la Riseholme, and Key Lime Pie," *PMLA* 104, no. 3 (May 1989): 340–47, sets up some useful parameters for reading cookbooks; I respectfully differ with some of her remarks on female solidarity in the kitchen. See the counterargument offered by Anne Goldman in "'I Yam What I Yam': Cooking, Culture, and Colonialism," in *De-Colonizing the Subject: The Politics of Gender in Women's Autobiography*, ed. Sidonie Smith and Julia Watson (Minneapolis: University of Minnesota Press, 1992), 169–95.

CHAPTER 2. Born a Slave, Died a Chef

Portions of this chapter have previously appeared in *African American Foodways*, edited by Anne Bower (2007), and *Gastronomica* 1, no. 4 (2001).

1. See Catherine Clinton, *The Plantation Mistress: Women's World in the Old South* (New York: Pantheon, 1983), and Gillian Brown, "Someone's in the Kitchen with Dinah: Domestic Politics in *Uncle Tom's Cabin*," *American Quarterly* 38 (1986): 668–74.

2. Kyla Wazana Tompkins as well as the late Vincent Woodard specifically address the metaphoric and near literal cannibalism practiced on African Americans, enslaved and otherwise. See Tompkins's pioneering *Racial Indigestion: Eating Bodies in the Nineteenth Century* (New York: New York University Press, 2011), and *Vincent Woodard, The Delectable Negro: Human Consumption and Homoeroticism within U.S. Slave Culture*, ed. Justin A. Joyce and Dwight A. McBride (New York: New York University Press, 2014).

3. Toni Tipton-Martin's *The Jemima Code: Two Centuries of African American Cookbooks* (Austin: University of Texas Press, 2015) refers frequently to the specter of Black women cooks haunting modern American cookery. See also Psyche A. Williams-Forson's *Building Houses Out of Chicken Legs: Black Women, Food, and Power* (Chapel Hill: University of North Carolina Press, 2006).

4. Kelley Fanto Deetz has discussed the difficulty of reconstructing the lives and work of early Black chefs whose recipes were recorded by their white owners, suggesting that the inclusion of African dishes in white-authored cookbooks was a "signifier of [whites'] socioeconomic class, national identity, and pride" (114). See "Stolen Bodies, Edible Memories: The Influence and Function of West African Foodways in the Early British Atlantic," in *The Routledge History of Food*, ed. Carol Helstosky

(New York: Routledge, 2015), 113–30. In his notes for his uncompleted gastronomica, Arturo Schomburg wrote "Bills of sale of slaves mentioning cooking ability," a fact of the slave trade Deetz discusses decades later.

5. The current Mount Vernon website provides information on Hercules, a history that would not have been promoted not that long ago. See http://www.mountvernon.org/digital-encyclopedia/article/hercules/. Other research revelatory of the life of Hercules includes Craig LeBan, "Hercules, Master of Cuisine, Slave of Washington," *Philadelphia Inquirer*, February 19, 2010, http://www.philly.com/philly/multimedia/20100219_Hercules__Master_of_cuisine__slave_of_Washington.html, and historian Ericka Armstrong Dunbar's study *Never Caught: The Washingtons' Relentless Pursuit of Their Runaway Slave, Ona Judge* (New York: Simon & Schuster, 2017), which provides detail and historical context.

6. See Annette Gordon-Reed, *The Hemingses of Monticello: An American Family* (New York: Norton, 2008), 489–90 and passim. Hemings honed his métier in Parisian kitchens, learning French at the same time.

7. Adrian Miller's *The President's Kitchen Cabinet: The Story of the African Americans Who Have Fed Our First Families, from the Washingtons to the Obamas* (Chapel Hill: University of North Carolina Press, 2017) fills in many gaps in the story of African Americans in presidential kitchens.

8. Although few cookery books by African Americans were published before 1914, a complete discussion of them would range beyond the boundaries of this chapter. They include *The Warm Springs Receipt Book* by E. T. Glover (1897), Franklyn H. Hall's *How to Make and Serve 100 Choice Broths and Soups* (1903) and *300 Ways to Cook & Serve Shellfish* (1901), Bertha Turner's *The Federation Cookbook* (1910), and Thomas Bivins's *The Southern Cookbook* (1912). See Doris Witt and David Lupton's bibliography in Witt, *Black Hunger: Food and the Politics of U.S. Identity* (Oxford: Oxford University Press, 1999), 221–28. The Witt and Lupton bibliography does not list Hall's 1903 volume, nor his *Standard American Culinary Encyclopedia*, which is listed as a previous publication on the title page of his *How to Make and Serve 100 Choice Broths and Soups*. (A copy of the encyclopedia does not appear to have survived.) Early works continue to be identified, as was the case with the Malinda Russell cookbook, which was rediscovered by culinary historian and bibliophile Janice B. Longone about a year after the Witt and Lupton bibliography appeared. See Molly O'Neill, "A 19th-Century Ghost Awakens to Redefine 'Soul,'" *New York Times*, November 21, 2007, http://www.nytimes.com/2007/11/21/dining/21cook.html. Danya Pilgrim's forthcoming study will address the lives and work of nineteenth-century Black hospitality entrepreneurs. Pilgrim, personal communication, July 20, 2017.

9. Anne Goldman's *Take My Word: Autobiographical Innovations of Ethnic American Working Women* (Berkeley: University of California, 1996) is an early affirmation of cookbooks as "nontraditional" autobiography.

10. Robert Roberts was born in South Carolina, and while he does not specifically address the issue of slavery, he details the possible hazards of employer-servant, if

not master-slave relations. Karen Hess, citing the research of Dan Strehl of the Los Angeles Public Library, affirms that Fisher was born a slave; see Fisher, *What Mrs. Fisher Knows about Southern Cooking*, ed. Karen L. Hess (Bedford, MA: Applewood, 1995), 76.

11. Foreman, "Manifest in Signs," 78.

12. See, for example, William L. Andrews, "Reunion in the Postbellum Slave Narrative: Frederick Douglass and Elizabeth Keckley," *Black American Literature Forum* 23, no. 1 (Spring 1989): 585–86.

13. I earlier addressed this idea of self-authentication in *We Wear the Mask*; see my discussion of William Wells Brown's *Clotel*, 85–86. For a discussion of enslaved Black chefs who never wrote a cookbook, see chapter 7, "The Negro Cooks Up His Past," 83, in this volume.

14. Malinda Russell, *A Domestic Cook Book: Containing a Careful Selection of Useful Receipts for the Kitchen*, edited by Janice Longone (1866; reprint, Ann Arbor, MI: William L. Clements Library, 2007), xi. Further references to the text are to this facsimile edition of Russell's cookbook. Longone noted that the earlier volumes by Roberts and Campbell could more precisely be referred to as "household management" guides (xi).

15. Harriet Wilson's autobiographical *Our Nig* was published just a few years earlier and similarly sought to earn funds to support a widowed mother and her child. Wilson, *Our Nig, or, Sketches from the Life of a Free Black*, ed. P. Gabrielle Foreman and Reginald H. Pitts (1859; reprint, London: Penguin, 2005).

16. The author expresses an apparently quixotic viewpoint, one noted by William Andrews in regard to other post–Civil War Black writers: "The postbellum narrator's attitude toward the slave past is . . . remarkably open to the proposition that something positive, something sustaining, could be gleaned from that past." "Reunion," 14. On the persistence of viewing the South as home, see Twitty, "Preface: The Old South," in *The Cooking Gene*, xi–xvii.

17. For information about the *True Northerner*, see "Chronicling America" on the Library of Congress's website, http://chroniclingamerica.loc.gov/lccn/sn85033781/. A perusal of the front page of the June 17, 1864, paper (the only one available and digitized) reveals numerous confirmations of the editorial orientation, including an article referring to the "blighting curse" of slavery.

18. Longone's introduction to Russell, *Cook Book*, vii.

19. Longone notes that President Andrew Jackson's library included not only *The Virginia Housewife* but also Robert Roberts's *House Servant's Directory*, attesting to the status both books held for households seeking to offer the highest level of hospitality. Longone in Russell, Cookbook (xi).

20. Fisher, *What Mrs. Fisher Knows*, 3.

21. California was admitted to the Union as a free state in 1849. Nevertheless, there were numerous cases of African Americans illegally brought into the state to work as slaves.

22. Frederick Douglass, *Narrative of the Life of Frederick Douglass, Written by Himself* (1845), reprinted in *Douglass: Autobiographies*, ed. Henry Louis Gates Jr. (New York: Library of America, 1994), 15.

23. See Hess, "Afterword," in Fisher, *What Mrs. Fisher Knows*, 76–94.

24. I have speculated that Fisher's "luck" could have turned on her possession of a light skin, bestowed by a Caucasian forebear. The story of Sally Hemings, Jefferson's longtime enslaved consort, provides a cautionary example in that some, but not all, members of her family were freed after Jefferson's death. See Gordon-Reed, "Epilogue," *Hemingses of Monticello*, 655–62.

25. See Darlene Clark Hine, "Rape and the Inner Lives of Southern Black Women: Thoughts on the Culture of Dissemblance," in *Southern Women: Histories and Identities*, ed. Virginia Bernhard, Betty Brandon, Elizabeth Fox-Genovese, and Theda Perdue (Columbia: University of Missouri Press, 1992), 177–89.

26. Booker T. Washington, founder of Tuskegee Institute (now University), published his best-selling autobiography, *Up from Slavery*, in 1901; for a facsimile edition see http://docsouth.unc.edu/fpn/washington/washing.html. See "There Is Probably No Subject More Important Than the Study of Food" in this volume.

27. D. J. Frienz [Dianna Seay], introduction to *Good Things to Eat: As Suggested by Rufus* (Jenks, OK: Howling at the Moon Press, 1999), n.p.

CHAPTER 3. "There Is Probably No Subject More Important Than the Study of Food"

Portions of this chapter have previously appeared in *The Common Reader* (May 8, 2015).

1. George Washington Carver, "Autobiography," 1897, reel 1, George Washington Carver Papers at Tuskegee Institute, Tuskegee, Alabama.

2. George Washington Carver, "Autobiography."

3. See the chapter "Divine Inspiration," 179–93 and passim, in Mark D. Hersey, *My Work Is That of Conservation: An Environmental Biography of George Washington Carver* (Athens: University of Georgia Press, 2011).

4. Moody's memoir, *Coming of Age in Mississippi*, is in its own way equally concerned with the role of food as a "field of action." See also my later chapter, "Civil Rights and Commensality."

5. Jennifer Jensen Wallach, "Dethroning the Deceitful Pork Chop: Food Reform at Tuskegee Institute," in *Dethroning the Deceitful Pork Chop: Rethinking African American Foodways* (Fayetteville: University of Arkansas Press, 2015), 166.

6. Linda McMurray, *George Washington Carver: Scientist and Symbol* (Oxford: Oxford University Press, 1981), 13. Mark D. Hersey notes that Jim Carver's death in 1883 left G. W. Carver with no known living relatives (*My Work Is Conservation*, 17). It is ironic, but perhaps unsurprising, that the "frail'" and bookish Carver would live until about his eightieth year (Carver's birth year is said to be about 1864).

7. Carver, quoted in Gary R. Kremer, *George Washington Carver in His Own Words* (Columbia: University of Missouri Press, 1987), 23.

8. Quoted in Kremer, *George Washington Carver*, 24. I have also read Carver's manuscript autobiography in the microform edition of his papers; readers interested in Carver's life will find the Kremer volume more accessible.

9. McMurray, *George Washington Carver*, 63, 24.

10. Carver's agricultural genius and Tuskegee's renown led to him being contacted by, among others, Germans pursuing cotton cultivation in East Africa. See Andrew Zimmerman, *Alabama in Africa: Booker T. Washington, the German Empire, and the Globalization of the New South* (Princeton, NJ: Princeton University Press, 2010), 181.

11. Rackham Holt, *George Washington Carver: An American Biography* (New York: Doubleday, Doran, 1943), 301. He was, as always, sporting a lapel flower.

12. In death they remained colleagues: Carver was interred on campus near his mentor and sometimes sparring partner Booker T. Washington.

13. In an introduction to the very first bulletin, *Feeding Acorns* (1898), Carver announced that in 1896–97 the Alabama legislature established a Tuskegee experiment station "with the view of educating and training colored students . . . in scientific agriculture" (4). See the digital Carver collection at Tuskegee University, http://archive.tuskegee.edu/archive/handle/123456789/192. All of Carver's bulletins, including the ones cited here, are available through this resource. A complete listing of Carver's bulletins may be accessed at http://archive.tuskegee.edu/archive/handle/123456789/337. I am indebted to Tuskegee University archivist Dana Chandler for his assistance with the digital archive.

14. In addition to the bulletins, Carver published numerous articles in various journals and gave many interviews. See McMurray, *George Washington Carver*, 78–79, for more details on the publication of the bulletins.

15. George Washington Carver, Bulletin no. 7: *Cotton Growing on Sandy Uplands Soils* (Tuskegee, AL: Tuskegee University, 1905), http://archive.tuskegee.edu/archive/handle/123456789/200.

16. See Rafia Zafar, "Recipes for Respect: Black Hospitality Entrepreneurs before World War I," in *African American Foodways*, ed. Anne L. Bower (Urbana: University of Illinois Press, 2007), 139–52.

17. Carver repeatedly refers to the "farmer's wife," although women were certainly farmers as well, if not as frequently heads of farms.

18. These recipes were repeated in other editions but are taken from Bulletin no. 5.

19. McMurray has noted that "few contemporaries grasped what he was really trying to say or do," *George Washington Carver*, 308.

20. McMurray, *George Washington Carver*, 306.

21. Thomas Monroe Campbell, *The Movable School Goes to the Negro Farmer* (1936; reprint, New York: Arno Press/New York Times, 1969), 82.

22. I deliberately here use "farmer and his wife," as that was invariably the locution used by Carver and his associates; that the farmer could be a woman—or that

the male could be versed in the domestic arts, as was Carver himself—generally went unacknowledged.

23. McMurray, *George Washington Carver*, 90.

24. To paraphrase Washington: while a community may not initially need someone who can parse Greek, a community would need someone who could fix wagons. Having those wagons would lead to a higher standard of living and eventually Greek instruction. Booker T. Washington, *Up from Slavery*, chapter 10, http://www.gutenberg.org/files/2376/2376-h/2376-h.htm, 217–18.

25. Martha Martin's *The Weed's Philosophy and Other Poems* was published in 1913. See https://archive.org/details/weedsphilosophyoooomartuoft, courtesy of the University of Toronto Libraries. (Carver added the exclamation point.)

26. Lamb's-quarters is in the *Chenopodium* family, much represented on restaurant tables these days by its chic cousin, quinoa. Carver originally wanted to be an artist and spent his first undergraduate years studying art at Simpson College in Iowa; one of his paintings, of a yucca plant, was exhibited at the 1893 Chicago Exposition.

27. Carver anticipated the STEAM movement of recent higher education planners: science, technology, engineering, art, and mathematics.

28. Alice Walker, "In Search of Our Mothers' Gardens: The Creativity of Black Women in the South," published in *Ms.*, May 1974; http://www.msmagazine.com/spring2002/walker.asp. Also available in the anthology by that title published in 1983 by Harcourt Brace.

29. On the subject of self-sufficiency, Carver overlaps with the pronouncements of Marcus Garvey and the Nation of Islam; the botanist, however, would likely aver that his methods could be used by all, even if initially aimed at the Black subsistence farmer.

30. Will Allen with Charles Wilson, *The Good Food Revolution: Growing Healthy Food, People, and Communities* (New York: Gotham, 2012), 100. Allen also quotes Carver as a model when he begins using red wiggler worms to create soil candy. He first had to learn how to take care of the little creatures: "'If you love it enough,' the agriculturalist George Washington Carver once wrote, 'anything will talk to you'" (118).

CHAPTER 4. Civil Rights and Commensality

1. Walt Whitman, "Song of Myself" (1892 version), sections 1, 19, 33. Available at The Poetry Foundation, https://www.poetryfoundation.org/poems/45477/song-of-myself-1892-version.

2. Langston Hughes, "I, Too," in *The Collected Poems of Langston Hughes*, ed. Arnold Rampersad and David Roessel (New York: Knopf, 1994), 46.

3. Moody began at a junior college, then transferred to Tougaloo and graduated in 1964. Walker began at Spelman but transferred to Sarah Lawrence College, from

which she graduated in 1965. Each young woman rebelled against the limitations of proper middle-class female behavior and performed various kinds of civil liberty work.

4. "It is dangerous to ignore the fact that uncertainty combined with competitiveness and rapid change always give a ruthless twist to selective patterns of hospitality." Douglas, "Standard Social Uses of Food," 36.

5. Anne Moody, *Coming of Age in Mississippi* (1968; reprint, New York: Delta, 2004).

6. Tea cakes, made from standard pantry ingredients, are a not-too-sweet small cake (or soft cookie). In a very poor household such as that of the Moodys', even common items such as butter and eggs were often not available.

7. See Rebecca Sharpless's study *Cooking in Other Women's Kitchens: Domestic Workers in the South, 1865–1960* (Chapel Hill: University of North Carolina Press, 2010) for ample documentation of such practices.

8. Ann Petry's best-selling novel *The Street* (1946), about a single mother's struggles in a harsh New York City, confirmed that African American poverty did not end with migration to the North, as I will discuss in my forthcoming essay, "Kitchenette UnBuilding."

9. Douglass, *Narrative*, 33.

10. Pierre Bourdieu, *Distinction: A Social Critique of the Judgement of Taste*, trans. Richard Nice (Cambridge, MA: Harvard University Press, 1984), 178.

11. Bourdieu's research for *Distinction* was conducted in 1960s France. If cast along lines of race or national origin, his research might tell a different story.

12. Douglas, "Standard Social Uses," 35.

13. Alice Walker, *Meridian* (1976; reprint, New York: Harvest Books, 2003).

14. See Mark Weiner, "Consumer Culture and Participatory Democracy: The Story of Coca-Cola during World War II," in *Food in the U.S.A.*, ed. Carole Counihan (New York: Routledge, 2002), 137.

15. Lauren S. Cardon, "From Black Nationalism to the Ethnic Revival: *Meridian's* Lynne Rabinowitz," *MELUS* 36, no. 30 (Fall 2001): 162.

16. See Lisa A. Heldke, *Exotic Appetites: Ruminations of a Food Adventurer* (New York: Routledge, 2003), and Susan Kalčik, "Ethnic Foodways in America: Symbol and the Performance of Identity," in Ethnic and Regional *Foodways in the United States: The Performance of Group Identity*, ed. Linda Keller Brown and Kay Mussell (Knoxville: University of Tennessee Press, 1984) for complementary perspectives on eating an outsider culture's food.

17. Cardon makes the argument that Walker asserts in her novel the importance of self-knowledge for truly revolutionary action, yet this critic may be too optimistic in her prediction of Lynne's eventual epiphany. "Black Nationalism," 180–81.

18. Ernest J. Gaines, *A Gathering of Old Men* (1983; reprint, New York: Vintage, 1984).

19. John Lowe, email to author, July 15, 2010.

20. Herman Beavers, *Wrestling Angels into Song: The Fictions of Ernest J. Gaines and James Alan McPherson* (Philadelphia: University of Pennsylvania Press, 1995), 7.

21. We never learn Snookum's given name.

22. Connie Eble explains in the newsletter of *Dictionary of American Regional English* (*DARE*) the word "praline"—that sweet candy known to all who visit New Orleans or Louisiana—is sometimes pronounced with a "metathesis," thus "plarine" (3). See http://dare.wisc.edu/sites/dare.wisc.edu/files/DARENEWS64.pdf.

23. Although Ramsay focuses on a different novel, she illuminates *Gathering* as well. See Courtney Ramsay, "Louisiana Foodways in Ernest Gaines's *A Lesson Before Dying*," *Louisiana Folklore* Miscellany (1995), reprinted at http://www.louisianafolklife.org/LT/Articles_Essays/main_misc_gaines_foodways.html.

24. The character Joseph Seaberry—a.k.a. "Rufe"—is the narrator here.

25. Mary Douglas, "Deciphering a Meal," *Daedalus* 101, no. 1 (Winter 1972): 66. "Those we know at meals we also know at drinks. The meal expresses close friendship. Those we only know at drinks we know less intimately. So long as this boundary matters to us (and there is no reason to suppose it will always matter) the boundary between drinks and meals has meaning."

26. Douglas, "Deciphering a Meal," 41. Because having drinks with someone attests to a level of respect in a racially divided milieu, we must pay additional attention to the difference between liquids and solids, as Mary Douglas would. Douglas asserts having drinks together, but not meals, implies one barrier is overcome but not others.

CHAPTER 5. The Signifying Dish

Portions of this chapter have previously appeared in *Feminist Studies* 25, no. 2 (1999), and *Voix Ethniques/Ethnic Voices* 2, no. 14 (1996). A shout out to Henry Louis Gates Jr.

1. John Egerton, *Southern Food: At Home, On the Road, In History* (1987; reprint, with a new author's preface, Chapel Hill: University of North Carolina Press, 1993), 16.

2. As one historian has written, "The spread of southern cooking to the North in our own day, like the spread of so much else in southern culture, has represented, above all, the triumph of its black component." Eugene D. Genovese, *Roll, Jordan, Roll: The World the Slaves Made* (1974; reprint, New York: Vintage, 1976), 543.

3. The popular Charleston [SC] Junior League's *Charleston Receipts* (Charleston, SC: Junior League of Charleston, 1950), a community cookbook organized by a white women's volunteer organization, has perpetuated these stereotypes for five decades. A "southern" cookbook, the renowned gentility of *Receipts* depends on the recipes, ingredients, and labor culled from the Blacks who labored in white kitchens. Cuisine elements deemed simple when offered elsewhere by African American practitioners here become classic when presented by white upper-middle-class employers. Sometimes thanked directly and sometimes not, the Black cooks are demeaned via quaint illustrations and even more quaint dialect; they become, in Patricia Yae-

ger's words, "edible labor." See Patricia Yaeger, "Edible Labor," *Southern Quarterly* 30, no. 2–3 (Winter–Spring 1992): 150–59, especially her remarks on the effaced Black cook/server (156). I have made an analogous observation, that of the politically vanquished become the rhetorically cannibalized; see Rafia Zafar, "The Proof of the Pudding: Of Haggis, Hasty Pudding, and Transatlantic Influence," *Early American Literature* 31 (1996): 133–49.

4. Patricia Turner, *Ceramic Uncles and Celluloid Mammies: Black Images and Their Influence on Culture* (Berkeley: University of California Press, 1995), 43. I direct readers again to Kyla Tompkins's excellent *Racial Indigestion*.

5. Much of culinary tradition and method is handed down orally, whatever the society. That cookery is "embodied knowledge," in Lisa M. Heldke's words, whether practiced by white or Black women, accounts for its denigrated status in a society that privileges pure reason; see Lisa Heldke, "Foodmaking as a Thoughtful Practice," in *Cooking, Eating, Thinking: Transformative Philosophies of Food*, ed. Deane W. Curtin and Lisa M. Heldke (Bloomington: Indiana University Press, 1992), 203–29, esp. 218–20. The doubly low status of Black women predicts their nearly subterranean level in U.S. society and, by way of a corollary, the belief in their gastronomic labors as unworthy of notice. Quandra Prettyman discusses Black women chefs Edna Lewis and Cleora Butler in addition to the Darden sisters and Vertamae Smart-Grosvenor; we arrive at some of the same conclusions. See Prettyman, "Come Eat at My Table: Lives with Recipes," *Southern Quarterly* 30, no. 2–3 (Winter–Spring 1992): 131–40.

6. As Doris (Smith) Witt has remarked, "The cookbook is a privileged textual site among blacks because of their overdetermined overrepresentation in American kitchens, both public and private" (26); she also discusses the mammy figure, with particular reference to turn-of-the-twentieth-century American culture (22–23). See Doris Smith, "In Search of Our Mothers' Cookbooks: Gathering African-American Culinary Traditions," *Iris*, Fall/Winter 1991, 22–27.

7. As Geneviève Fabre and Robert O'Meally observe, such African American *lieux des mémoires* "prompt both the processes of imaginative recollection and the historical consciousness. . . . [They] stand at the nexus of personal and collective memory." Introduction to Fabre and O'Meally, eds., *History and Memory in African-American Culture* (Oxford: Oxford University Press, 1994), 7.

8. Vertamae Smart-Grosvenor, *Vibration Cooking* (1970; reprint with revisions, New York: Ballantine, 1986, 1991); in-text references are to the most recent edition, unless otherwise noted. Carole and Norma Jean Darden's *Spoonbread and Strawberry Wine* (New York: Doubleday, 1978) is also in paper, but I have used the original hardcover. The publication history of these two works attests to their continued popularity: *Spoonbread* has been in print pretty much continuously since its first publication; *Vibration Cooking* is now in its third edition. Much anecdotal evidence indicates that hardcover first editions of *Vibration Cooking* are often borrowed from, and never returned to, their original owners.

9. See, for example, Bertha Turner, ed., *The Federation Cookbook: A Collection of Tested Recipes, Contributed by the Colored Women of the State of California* (Pasadena, 1910).

10. Freda DeKnight, *The Ebony Cookbook: A Date with a Dish* (Chicago: Johnson, 1962); National Council of Negro Women, *Historical Cookbook of the American Negro* (Washington, D.C.: Corporate Press, 1958).

11. Emblematic of a kind of ripple effect, similar celebrations of one's origins—as well as one's political activism—arose in other groups. In terms of cultural origins, the impetus to celebrate one's identity came to be known in the 1970s as the "ethnic revival"; along with this rise in various Americans' perceptions of themselves as "Italian" or "Greek" came a corresponding interest in ethnic cookbooks and restaurants. (Ethnic cookbooks, as such, appeared well before the 1970s.) In terms of a political affiliation expressed through an alternative venue, cookbooks and/or food also became a way to express a certain lifestyle and/or social change. One volume that provides examples of both impulses is Ita Jones's *The Grubbag: An Underground Cookbook* (New York: Vintage, 1971), which grew out of a column in the Liberation News Service; Jones refers to her upbringing in Texas and her search for ethnic origins. For discussions of such politically oriented endeavors, see Warren Belasco, *Appetite for Change: How the Counterculture Took On the Food Industry*, updated edition (Ithaca, NY: Cornell University Press, 1989, 1993) and Curtin and Heldke, *Cooking, Eating, Thinking*.

12. Fewer than fifteen books were published by Black presses in the first part of the 1960s, while about 160 books by similar firms appeared between 1970 and 1974. Donald Franklin Joyce's research on the Black press demonstrates this sharp rise in the number and output of Black-owned presses post-1960; he also discusses the exchanges and competition between white- and Black-owned publishers. See Joyce, *Gatekeepers of Black Culture* (Westport, CT: Greenwood, 1983), esp. 78–79, 147.

13. Ruth L. Gaskins, *A Good Heart and a Light Hand: Ruth L. Gaskins' Collection of Traditional Negro Recipes* (Annandale, VA: Turnpike, 1968). Quandra Prettyman's essay "Come Eat at My Table" and Howard Paige's *Aspects of Afro-American Cookery* (Southfield, MI: Aspects, 1987) each provide bibliographies in their publications, as do Doris Witt's *Black Hunger* and Toni Tipton-Martin's lovingly illustrated and annotated guide, *The Jemima Code*. The David Walker Lupton African American Cookbook Collection at the University of Alabama showcases a dedicated collector's riches: https://www.lib.ua.edu/collections/the-david-walker-lupton-african-american-cookbook-collection/.

14. For an excellent discussion of how "soul food" came to be identified with Black folks, see Doris Witt, *Black Hunger*, 79–101 passim.

15. Despite the growing numbers of Black Americans in the professional and middle classes, the percentage of Black poor remains far too large for any American to feel complacent. The presidency of Barack Obama did not erase the educational and wealth gaps between white and Black, much less health disparities. Nonetheless,

there has long been an identifiable middle or upper class in African America: see Jessica B. Harris's "Heirloom Recipes from a Southern Family: A Big-Flavored Meal in the African-American Tradition," *Food and Wine*, February 1991, for an overview of Black class differences in the kitchen.

16. Think, for example, of the "high class" volumes of Julia Child, with their implication that the cook will spend hours in the kitchen, using expensive ingredients; note again Smart-Grosvenor's above-quoted remark on this implied distinction between "white" and "black" food": "White folks act like . . . there is some weird mystique [about food]" (3).

17. Exceptions could be found in the collectively authored community or "charity" cookbooks: volumes compiled by a group of women whose initial motives were often financial (to rebuild a church, or to raise funds for relief organizations), but whose final products could speak to both individual desires for recognition and an acknowledgment of woman's worth. See Marion Bishop, "Speaking Sisters: Relief Society Cookbooks and Mormon Culture," in *Recipes for Reading: History, Stories, Community Cookbooks*, ed. Anne L. Bower (Amherst: University of Massachusetts Press, 1997), 89–104. In the same volume, Ann Romines's essay, "Growing Up with the Methodist Cookbooks" (75–88), attests that such community cookbooks were the most-used texts her family owned. Bower's fine anthology collects a number of essays on community cookbooks—as autobiographies, cultural histories, and women's alternative media.

18. I have elsewhere discussed Smart-Grosvenor's diasporic peregrinations in "Verta Mae Reverses the Middle Passage," an unpublished paper delivered at the Modern Language Association meeting, December 1999.

19. Goldman, *Take My Word*, 42.

20. Goldman also finds the irreverence and sass of Smart-Grosvenor to be similar to Hurston's; see *Take My Word*, 47–49.

21. Doris Witt's *Black Hunger* cogently discusses the evolution of Smart-Grosvenor's volume over its three editions and two-plus decades. See also Psyche Williams-Forson's excellent foreword to the latest edition of *Vibration Cooking: or, The Travel Notes of a Geechee Girl* (Athens: University of Georgia Press, 2011), xii–xxxii.

22. In a well-known moment of gastronomic essentialism, the fictional Chloe of *Uncle Tom's Cabin* exclaims: "Look at my great black stumpin hands. Now, don't ye think dat de Lord must have meant me to make de pie-crust, and you [Mrs. Shelby, the slave's "mistress"] to stay in the parlor?" Harriet Beecher Stowe, *Uncle Tom's Cabin* (1852; reprint, New York: Harper Classics, 1965), 27.

23. Doris Witt's "'My Kitchen Was the World': Vertamae Smart Grosvenor's Geechee Diaspora," in *Black Hunger*, refers to Smart-Grosvenor's "The Kitchen Crisis" and *Thursdays and Every Other Sunday Off* as specifically concerned with the status of domestic servants.

24. See Anne Goldman's "'I Yam What I Yam'," esp. 171–73, which takes issue with

Susan J. Leonardi's invocation of a female-centered, cross-class recipe exchange. See Leonardi, "Recipes for Reading," for the origins of this debate.

25. I discuss Alice B. Toklas in conjunction with her fellow cookbook-memoirist, Edna Lewis, in the final chapter. Her expatriate social set and culinary doings are the well-known subjects of *The Alice B. Toklas Cookbook* (1954; reprint, New York: Harper Perennial, 1984).

26. Toklas may have had more entrée into French society than Smart-Grosvenor, by virtue of being white, but the African American counts wealthy people among her set as well. On the other hand, Smart-Grosvenor was not immune from heterosexism: in the preface to the second edition (1986), Smart-Grosvenor decides not to excise a homophobic remark. In the most recent printing (1991), the offensive sentence—"I wouldn't pay no faggot six hundred dollars to dress me up like a fool" (page 152 in the 1986 edition)—is expunged.

27. So sure is Smart-Grosvenor of her value as an author and person, rather than a "mere" cook, that she includes an entire chapter of her correspondence—a move Robert Stepto might refer to as self-authenticating.

28. Those of us who cook from the books we read will notice at least one divergence in philosophy, if not in method. While Toklas and Smart-Grosvenor share a respect for their audience, cooks' expertise, and common sense, Smart-Grosvenor insists "I never measure or weigh anything. I cook by vibration. . . . The amount of salt and pepper you want to use is your own business" (3).

29. In this, Smart-Grosvenor can be said to anticipate Alice Walker's well-known claiming of Black women foremothers in *In Search of Our Mother's Gardens*, esp. 3–14.

30. See Zafar, "Verta Mae Reverses."

31. Freda DeKnight, *A Date with a Dish: A Cook Book of American Negro Recipes* (1948; revised and reprinted as *The Ebony Cookbook: A Date with a Dish*, Chicago: Johnson, 1962, 1973). Thanks to Doris Witt for helping me sort out the dates.

32. References to *A Date with a Dish* and several other Black cookbooks are absent in the 1992 preface, although she does refer to John Pinderhughes. Smart-Grosvenor may not have been aware of the history of Black cookbooks, in part due to the relative obscurity of many such works. Witt and Lupton list about forty Black-authored cookbooks before 1970; a good number were published by small presses or brought out by the authors themselves.

33. Although it may not need saying, I'll note it anyway—the positions I sketch out here, between individual and community, between Smart-Grosvenor and the Dardens, are not absolute; elements of each outlook are found in both texts. Perhaps it's best to say that each cookbook emphasizes a different authorial stance.

34. The term is Clifford Geertz's; for amplification, see "Thick Description: Toward the Interpretative Theory of Culture," in *The Interpretation of Cultures: Selected Essays* (New York: Basic Books, 1973), 3–30.

35. Susan Kalcik and others explore the transmission of ethnic identity through food. Elizabeth and Paul Rozin have noted that flavor may function symbolically: having ethnic "tastes" places an individual within a specific group. Similarly, foods with a particular taste identify themselves as belonging to a particular community. E. Rozin and P. Rozin, "Some Surprisingly Unique Characteristics of Human Food Preferences," in *Food in Perspective: Proceedings of the Third International Conference on Ethnological Food Research, Cardiff, Wales,* ed. Alexander Fenton and Trefor Owen (Edinburgh: John Donald Publishers, 1981), 243–52.

36. Irma McClaurin reminds me that the book was published in 1978, and so before the current suburbanization of the Black middle class. That *Spoonbread* remains in print, and was even adapted into a play in the 1990s, may speak to its continuing, *reinvented* appeal as a nostalgia item for the contemporary Black bourgeoisie.

37. I will return to this idea in the chapter on Edna Lewis, using the West African symbol of *sankofa*: that to go forward one must look behind.

38. The food pages of *Essence* attest to the bind between the need for quick, easy meals and the desire for "heritage" recipes; thanks again to Irma McClaurin for reminding me of the continuing, if changing, significance of Sunday dinner.

39. Chitlins, or chitterlings, are pig intestines; they "are testament to the downhome doctrine that nothing in the hog is inedible." See Rick Bragg, "Atlanta Journal: A Delicacy of the Past Is a Winner at Drive-In," *New York Times*, November 10, 1996, https://www.nytimes.com/1996/11/10/us/a-delicacy-of-the-past-is-a-winner-at -drive-in.html. Two decades on, the chitlins remain: https://thisisitbbq.com/camp _creek_full_service_orders/index.php?act=category&cid=33.

40. See Lena Williams, "Preparing Soul Food Can Now Be as Easy as Opening a Can," *New York Times*, May 26, 1993, https://www.nytimes.com/1993/05/26/garden /preparing-soul-food-can-now-be-as-easy-as-opening-a-can.html.

41. Quoted in Bragg, "Delicacy of the Past," 20. Latter-day proscriptions against pork by Muslims and others in Black America wishing to separate themselves from a slave past may also have effected the turn away from pork products. See the reference to the turn against pork in the passage on New Year's Day in *Vibration Cooking*, discussed below.

42. The avoidance of certain foods on the part of younger people speaks in part to a related desire to distance themselves from hardship and social ostracization. See my discussion of Bourdieu and his concept of the "foods of necessity," relevant to Anne Moody, in the previous chapter.

43. The Dardens built on their fame, at one time running two restaurants named "Spoonbread" in Harlem, New York. Vertamae Smart-Grosvenor also used *Vibration* to leverage her presence in the media and publishing worlds.

44. "[In 1808] Congress finally prohibited the slave trade. Absalom Jones and other Black preachers began delivering annual thanksgiving sermons on New Year's

Day, the date of the prohibition of trade and also the date of Haitian independence in 1804." Gary B. Nash, *Forging Freedom*, quoted in Ntozake Shange, *If I Can Cook / You Know God Can* (Boston: Beacon, 1998), 6.

45. Howard Paige, informal talk, "African American Emancipation Day Celebrations," Greenfield Village Museum, Dearborn, Michigan, August 1991. See Karen L. Hess's "Hoppin John and Other Bean Pilaus of the African Diaspora" in *The Carolina Rice Kitchen: The African Connection* (Columbia: University of South Carolina Press, 1992), 92–110.

46. Compare my observation with a similar one of Doris (Smith) Witt's, on the handling of greens by the same cook: "Grosvenor manages to recreate the social context of recipe exchange, yet she simultaneously refuses to give us anything but thoroughly imprecise and unscientific suggestions on what to, and not to, do with greens. She offers a nuanced analysis of the social forces which come into play in the economy of recipe exchange." Smith, "In Search of Our Mothers' Cookbooks," 25.

47. Surprisingly, although intent on recapturing the exact tastes and smells of the past, the Darden sisters show less resistance to modernization.

48. Vertamae Smart-Grosvenor, *Black Atlantic Cooking* (Upper Saddle River, NJ: Prentice Hall, 1990).

49. Harris, "Heirloom Recipes," 50.

50. I refer here to Bourdieu's *amor fati*, the "predestined" taste for the food of the past.

51. Jessica B. Harris, *Iron Pots and Wooden Spoons: Africa's Gifts to New World Cooking* (New York: Atheneum, 1989), 15, 11.

52. I surmise from the few student hands raised in response to my query, "Do you know what pot likker is?" that the practice is fading. I, on the other hand, having lived with a grandmother who was raised in part in a southern Black community, was frequently admonished to drink my pot likker.

53. As raw kale salads are now a restaurant staple, this assertion doesn't carry the humorous weight it once did.

54. Cookbooks in the late 1990s regularly suggested smoked turkey wings as substitutions for pork in various dishes; baked macaroni and cheese, a staple at Black American family functions, cannot be traced back to West Africa.

55. For a discussion of how ethnic groups persist as such and yet change in composition and style, see Fredrik Barth, Introduction to *Ethnic Groups and Boundaries: The Social Organization of Culture Difference* (Boston: Little, Brown, 1969), 9–38. A contemporary expression of the "changing same" (to borrow from LeRoi Jones) or the reinvention and revival of Black cultural mores, can be seen in contemporary Black foodways such as Bryant Terry's *Vegan Soul Food Kitchen: Fresh, Healthy, and Creative African American Cuisine* (Cambridge, MA: Da Capo, 2009).

56. The significance of early eating habits in creating a bedrock, ethnic self has been noted by various researchers: "Foodways seem particularly resistant to change. . . . It has been suggested that this is because the earliest-formed layers of

culture, such as foodways, are the last to erode." Susan Kalčik discusses this phenomenon in her essay, "Ethnic Foodways in America"; see esp. 39. See also Julie A. Mennella, Coren P. Jagnow, and Gary K. Beauchamp, "Prenatal and Postnatal Flavor Learning by Human Infants," *Pediatrics* 107, no. 6 (2001): E88.

57. Vivian Nun Halloran suggests that novels can function as museums as well as bricks and mortar. See Halloran, "Introduction: Novels as Museums in a Postmodern Age," in *Exhibiting Slavery: The Caribbean Postmodern Novel as Museum* (Charlottesville: University of Virginia Press, 2009), 1–20.

58. See the writings of Jessica B. Harris, John Pinderhughes's *Family of the Spirit Cookbook: Recipes and Remembrances from African-American Kitchens* (New York: Simon & Schuster, 1990), and Cleora Butler's *Cleora's Kitchens and Eight Decades of Great American Food: The Memoir of a Cook* (Tulsa, OK: Council Oak Books, 1985). Other more recent books display similar literary/historical/culinary instincts. Although each presents food and its role in the author's life differently, all the cooks choose to collect, compile, and record recipes taken from family, travels, friends, or an individual career as chef and caterer, and all take care to explain why one might want to conflate a cookbook with a historical or personal narrative.

CHAPTER 6. Elegy or *Sankofa*?

Portions of this chapter have previously appeared in *MELUS* 38, no. 4 (Winter 2013).

1. In 2010 the Library of Congress announced that, following a period of public comment and discussion within the library itself, the subject heading "Cookbooks" would be established as both a topical subject heading and a genre/form heading. See "Revision of Headings for Cooking and Cookbooks: Library of Congress Decisions and Cooking and Cookbooks," https://www.loc.gov/catdir/cpso/cooking3.pdf; Gretchen L. Hoffman, "How are Cookbooks Classified in Libraries? An Examination of LCSH and LCC," *North American Symposium on Knowledge Organization* 4, no. 1 (2013), http://journals.lib.washington.edu/index.php/nasko/article/view/14650. Thanks to Cheryl Holland, Washington University librarian, for these references; personal communication, July 2016. On the hidden biases of "neutral" catalog classifications, see also Gretchen L. Hoffman, "What's the Difference between Soul Food and Southern Cooking? The Classification of Cookbooks in American Libraries," in Wallach, *Dethroning the Deceitful Pork Chop*, 88–103.

2. The Library of Congress cataloguing change noted above, from cookbooks as an object of study as artifacts to the inclusion of cookbooks as a specific literary genre, acknowledges this shift from studying cookbooks as records of how individuals and cultures ate and prepared food, to a more encompassing field that looks at the way these compendia are structured and read in relation to literary history and criticism. This chapter joins this relatively recent focus on cookbooks as writerly texts.

3. As Susan Leonardi has identified, "A recipe is, then, an embedded discourse, and like other embedded discourses, it can have a variety of relationships with its frame, or its bed." "Recipes for Reading," 340.

4. As Bower wrote in her introduction to *Recipes for Reading*, there are various "ways in which 'nonliterary' texts can be read and valued. In turn, increasing awareness of the processes at work in nonliterary texts may inform new readings of the 'literary'" (14). In another essay, Bower quotes noted culinary historian Janice Longone saying she reads cookbooks like novels. See Longone, "Romanced by Cookbooks," *Gastronomica* 4, no. 2 (May 2004): 35–42.

5. A point the writer Monique Truong responds to in her novel *The Book of Salt* (Boston: Houghton Mifflin, 2003). Toklas's portraits of domestic workers frequently demean or patronize their subjects.

6. Edna Lewis, *The Taste of Country Cooking* (New York: Knopf, 1976), v. Subsequent references will be given parenthetically within the text.

7. The M. F. K. Fisher edition of Toklas's work, to which I refer throughout in parenthetical citations, drops the original title's spelling of "Cook Book." In this chapter, however, I will use the earlier locution.

8. David E. Sutton, *Remembrance of Repasts: An Anthropology of Food and Memory* (London: Berg, 2001), 168.

9. Traci Kelly's contention that "the culinary autobiography can be a site of multiple textual assertions" (267), and her discussion elsewhere, supports this idea of cookbooks operating in multiple genres—and by extension my claim that they may also operate as elegies. See Kelly, "If I Were a Voodoo Priestess: Women's Culinary Autobiographies," in *Kitchen Culture in America: Popular Representations of Food, Gender, and Race*, ed. Sherrie A. Inness (Philadelphia: University of Pennsylvania Press, 2001), 251–70.

10. Anne Bower states that cookbooks "form a genre governed by distinct codes and conventions" ("Cooking Up Stories," in *Recipes for Reading*, 29). See also the Library of Congress revised subject headings on cooking and cookbooks.

11. Woolf pondered whether her novels should have "a new name ... elegy?" Quoted in Christine Froula, "Mrs. Dalloway's Postwar Elegy: Women, War, and the Art of Mourning," *Modernism/modernity* 9, no. 1 (2002): 125–63, quotation on 125.

12. Christel Temple discusses the dissemination of the concept, notably its burgeoning resurgence in the United States. In the African American diaspora the word has become a synonym for a return to, or memory of, one's heritage. Temple, "The Emergence of Sankofa Practice in the United States: A Modern History," *Journal of Black Studies* 41, no. 1 (2010): 127.

13. M. H. Abrahams and Geoffrey Galt Harpham, *A Glossary of Literary Terms*, 8th ed. (Boston: Wadsworth, 2005), 77.

14. Jahan Ramazani, *Poetry of Mourning: The Modern Elegy from Hardy to Heaney* (Chicago: University of Chicago Press, 1994), 175; Max Cavitch, *American Elegy: The*

Poetry of Mourning from the Puritans to Whitman (Minneapolis: University of Minnesota Press, 2007), 2.

15. Cavitch, *American Elegy*, 3.

16. Diane Tye recalls "handwritten recipes are now almost the only remaining material legacy of my grandmother, who was barely literate." Tye, *Baking as Biography* (Montreal: McGill–Queen's University Press, 2010), 35.

17. Neither Ramazani nor Cavitch limit themselves to male authors, for they each seek to expand and deepen the parameters of what constitutes the elegy.

18. Schenck concludes that "the female elegist . . . protests final separation by insisting upon not only the difficulty of severing substantial relations, but the potential for achieving identity by preserving those very relations in a kind of continuous present" (24). See Celeste M. Schenck, "Feminism and Deconstruction: Reconstructing the Elegy," *Tulsa Studies in Women's Literature* 5, no. 1 (1986): 13–27. Lewis illuminates this point by her invocation of a continuum between a past Freetown and a present African American community.

19. Caren Kaplan, "Resisting Autobiography: Out-Law Genres and Transnational Feminist Subjects," in *Women, Autobiography, Theory: A Reader*, ed. Sidonie Smith and Julia Watson (Madison: University of Wisconsin Press, 1998), 208–16.

20. The 1993 film *Sankofa*, directed by the Ethiopian-born American director Haile Gerima, concerns a Black American model on location in Ghana who is mysteriously transported to the slave forts and subsequently to an American plantation.

21. Of course, elegy, in a cookbook, partakes of memoir—for memoir as a genre is relevant, too. The first-person accounts that make up memoirs do not simply recall an individual's life and experience but their interaction with their time period and others who lived then. Thus memoirs can be, but are not necessarily, elegiac in the sense of mourning—although they often do memorialize or recapture an era passed.

22. Carol J. Adams, *The Sexual Politics of Meat: A Feminist-Vegetarian Critical Theory*, 10th anniversary ed. (New York: Continuum, 2000).

23. The close parallels between Toklas's cookbook and Stein's writing have been discussed by several authors. One example can be found in Janet Malcolm, *Two Lives: Gertrude and Alice* (New Haven, CT: Yale University Press, 2007), 5.

24. In "A Word with the Cook," Toklas says she "wrote [*the Cook Book*] for America" but hopes it will find its place "in British kitchens too" (n.p.).

25. Toklas recalls that in the country "our French cook [taught] me to murder by smothering" (39), insisting that beheading birds was barbarous.

26. Carol Adams's insights about the alignment of patriarchy and meat eating do not sufficiently account for Toklas's generic experiment. Perhaps that is why Adams mentions the "Murder in the Kitchen" chapter only in passing (103).

27. Anna Linzie has pointed to Toklas's words as "obscure references to the killing of humans going on all around her" (160). Linzie, *The True Story of Alice B. Toklas: A Study of Three Autobiographies* (Iowa City: University of Iowa Press, 2006).

28. See also Toklas's *What Is Remembered* (New York: Holt, 1963). For a longer discussion of Toklas's relationship with her Jewish heritage, see Zafar, "Elegy and Remembrance in the Cookbooks of Alice B. Toklas and Edna Lewis," *MELUS* 38, no. 4 (Winter 2013): 32–35.

29. As Ramazani has said, "The modern elegy more radically violates previous generic norms than did earlier phases of elegy. . . . [It becomes] sometimes even antiliterary" (*Poetry of Mourning*, 2). Such a conceptualization could encompass cookbooks that recall and remember the dead rather than grieve for them.

30. Stein and Toklas left Bilignin in 1943, moving to Culoz until the end of 1944. At that point they returned to Paris. Lynn Weiss, personal communication, May 1, 2012.

31. Eric Asimov and Kim Severson, "Edna Lewis, 89, Dies; Wrote Cookbooks That Revived Refined Southern Cuisine," *New York Times*, February 2, 2006.

32. Lewis refers to guinea fowl as an animate link to Africa, rarely eaten; black-eyed peas and sorghum, she notes, have African origins as well (159, 174, 255). See also Jessica B. Harris, *High on the Hog: A Culinary Journey from Africa to America* (New York: Bloomsbury, 2011), xi–xx. Multiple extant photographs of Lewis in African and African-inspired clothing underscore the link she made between the present, the American past, and the African diaspora.

CHAPTER 7. The Negro Cooks Up His Past

Thanks to Jess Krug for pointing me to the perfect title. We nod of course to Schomburg's "The Negro Digs Up His Past, "in *The New Negro*, ed. Alain Locke (1925; reprint, New York: Atheneum, 1970). I also thank Jess for the direction to Stephan Palmié's epiphany, "What I do see today is that the notion of such a [spectral Africanist] presence in my life has levels of significance not exhausted in the literalism implied by such terms as *belief, plausibility,* or *rationality.*" Palmié, "Evidence and Presence, Spectral and Other," in *Wizards and Scientists: Explorations in Afro-Cuban Modernity and Tradition* (Durham, NC: Duke University Press, 2002), 1–38 (quotation on 3), following my remark that I felt like I was channeling Schomburg.

1. Were it not for an appendix to her book about African Americans and food, *Black Hunger*, in which scholar Doris Witt teamed up with bibliographer Richard Lupton to produce a chronology of African American–authored cookery books since the nineteenth century, I would be unaware of Schomburg's plans. The manuscript itself was titled by an unknown librarian. My thanks to Doris Witt, who has been a great colleague and pathmaker; I regret never having been able to meet the late Mr. Lupton, a noted bibliophile in his own right.

2. Current studies of Schomburg do not refer to any interest Schomburg had in cuisine, whether personally or academically. See, for example, Elinor Des Verney Sinnette, *Arthur Alfonso Schomburg: Black Bibliophile and Collector* (Detroit: New

York Public Library/Wayne State University Press, 1989); Vanessa K. Valdés, *Diasporic Blackness: The Life and Times of Arturo Alfonso Schomburg* (Albany: State University of New York Press, 2017); New York Public Library, *The Legacy of Arthur A. Schomburg: A Celebration of the Past, a Vision for the Future*, Exhibition at the Schomburg Center for Research in Black Culture, October 23, 1986–March 28, 1987 (New York: NYPL Schomburg Center for Research in Black Culture, 1988). One exception is Jesse Hoffnung-Garskoff's "The World of Arturo Alfonso Schomburg," in *The Afro-Latin@ Reader: History and Culture in the United States* (Durham, NC: Duke University Press, 2010), 70–91. Lance Thomas (Schomburg's great-grandson), personal communication, July 24, 2017; Dean Schomburg to Maira Liriano, personal communication, February 19, 2015.

3. Arthur Schomburg, "['Cookbook',]" 1. The manuscript is untitled and unsigned, with only the penciled notation "[cookbook]" on the first page, and is included in a folder identified as containing Schomburg's own writings. Arthur A. Schomburg Papers, "Writings by Arthur A. Schomburg," box 12, folder 2, microfilm reel 9/10, Schomburg Center for Research in Black Culture, New York Public Library. All parenthetical references within the text are to this document. Following page 20 of the manuscript and preceding a recipe for "Gumbo of Okra or Filee" is a handwritten page of notes; the script closely resembles the handwriting in Schomburg's letters and manuscripts. Other internal evidence—specifically, the December 1930 death of W. H. Cohen, Schomburg's friend—places the manuscript's initial composition no later than 1930. Subsequent references will be made parenthetically and refer to the original manuscript's pagination.

4. Doris Witt points us to John Brown Childs, "Afro-American Intellectuals and the People's Culture," *Journal of Theory and Society* 13 (1984): 69–90, for an early recognition of Schomburg's loving task. See Witt, *Black Hunger*, 176.

5. Schomburg, "The Negro Digs Up His Past," 237.

6. Sinnette, *Arthur Alfonso Schomburg*, 232–33. Laura Helton has recently discovered a manifest of Schomburg's holdings at the Fisk University archives; I look forward to perusing this listing when it is available for study. Maira Liriano and Steven Fullop worked with me to identify what books on foodways might have been in the collection at the time of Schomburg's death.

7. This may also have to do with the much-discussed, if sometimes overemphasized, split between a Du Boisian emphasis on intellectual achievement and a Washingtonian belief that vocational education should proceed and then empower social mobility.

8. The copy of Hearn's *Creole Cooking* available online via HathiTrust is a scan of the New York Public Library's volume stamped "The New York Public Library 805123A Astor, Lenox and Tilden Foundations R 1935 L." A handwritten entry alongside the first page of the introduction indicates it was a gift from a Mr. Gourley in 1935—but a specific branch is not identified.

9. Contemporary African American culinary historian Jessica B. Harris has frequently noted this phenomenon of a two-tiered cuisine throughout her career; see her salute to "the juncture of two Black culinary traditions: that of the Big House and that of the rural South," *Iron Pots and Wooden Spoons*, xxi. Schomburg predicted the revival of what would be called soul food in the 1960s. See Witt, *Black Hunger*, and Tracey N. Poe, "The Origins of Soul Food in Black Urban Identity: Chicago, 1915–1947," *American Studies International* 42, no. 2 (February 1999): 4–33. Pierre Bourdieu, of course, would point to the "taste of necessity."

10. Leland Ferguson, *Uncommon Ground: Archaeology and Early African America, 1650–1800* (Washington, D.C.: Smithsonian Books, 1992), 107.

11. See Judith Ann Carney and Richard Nicholas Rosomoff, *In the Shadow of Slavery: Africa's Botanical Legacy in the Atlantic World* (Berkeley: University of California Press, 2010), as well as Carney's first book, *Black Rice: The Origins of Rice Cultivation in the Americas* (Cambridge, MA: Harvard University Press, 2001). See also, for example, Hess, *Carolina Rice Kitchen*.

12. Such omissions remain perplexing, especially in light of Vanessa K. Valdés's recent study, *Diasporic Blackness*, underscoring Schomburg's active engagement with his Puerto Rican and Latin heritage. Valdés details Schomburg's "actively laid claim to the richness of the histories and cultures of the Spanish-speaking world" (4). See also her discussion of Schomburg's *cronicas*, 72–79.

13. Cohen's middle initial was I, not W; see Rachel Frantz, *African American Business Leaders and Entrepreneurs* (New York: Facts on File, 2004).

14. See "Born a Slave, Died a Chef," chapter 2 in this volume.

15. The Fraunces Tavern Museum refers to his origins as "a mystery," with no mention of earlier allegations of African ancestry. See http://www.frauncestavernmuseum .org/samuel-fraunces/?rq=Samuel%20Fraunces. George Washington's Mount Vernon historical museum has a website page on Fraunces (https://www.mountvernon .org/library/digitalhistory/digital-encyclopedia/article/samuel-fraunces/) and also does not address his ancestry, while citing Douglas R. Egerton's *Death or Liberty: African Americans and Revolutionary America* (Oxford: Oxford University Press, 2009), which refers to Fraunces as of "mixed" ancestry.

16. Arthur Schomburg, "Our Pioneers," *New York Amsterdam News*, August 1, 1936. Fraunces's African ancestry was recently asserted by Adrian Miller. See Miller, *President's Kitchen Cabinet*, 35–36.

17. Without the assistance of Maira Liriano, associate chief librarian of the Schomburg Center, the mysteries of the center's book holdings would have remained nearly impenetrable. I am indebted to her, and to retired librarian Diana Lachantere, for their assistance in decoding what clues to Schomburg's intentions exist. Rebecca Federman, curator for the New York Public Library's cookbook collection, has also been generous with her time and knowledge, not to mention good-humored.

18. Both a Dan and a Bill Singleton are referred to; it's not clear whether these are two different chefs or whether a typo has one man with two different first names. Mordecai Johnson was the first Howard University president of African descent; installed in 1926, he served for thirty-four years. http://www.howard.edu/library /reference/cybercamps/camp2001/studentwebs/shayna/default.html.

19. The language of the listing, "Half moon pies . . . especially delicious when . . ." brings to mind Carver's *Forty-Three Ways to Save the Wild Plum Crop*. Although the date of acquisition cannot be established, the Schomburg Center owns an original copy, a.k.a. *Tuskegee Bulletin* 34 (April 1917).

20. Like Augustus Jackson, Crum is credited with inventing a food item that already existed. Perhaps it is more accurate to claim him as a popularizer. See Myra B. Young Armstead, *"Lord, Don't Take Me in August": African Americans in Newport and Saratoga Springs, 1870–1930* (Urbana: University of Illinois Press, 1999), 22–23, on Crum and George Downing, another well-known caterer to elite whites in Saratoga and New York City alike.

21. Carrie Alberta Lyford, *A Book of Recipes for the Cooking School* (Hampton, VA: Hampton Normal and Agricultural Institute, 1921). Thanks to Doris Witt and Ralph Lupton for this reference.

22. Natalie Scott, *Mirations and Miracles of Mandy: Some Favorite Louisiana Recipes* (New Orleans: Robert True, 1929) and Betty Benton Patterson, *Mammy Lou's Cookbook* (New York: Robert McBride, 1931) each regretfully invoke the lost era of unlettered Black cooks who devoted themselves to their white families; eerily, each book relies on a "composite" chef rather than identifying specific cooks. Marcia Chatelain "refers to the interchangeable nature of Black cooks, as far as their white employers were concerned"; she cites a later edition of Scott's work, titled *Mandy's Favorite Louisiana Recipes*. See Chatelain, "Black Women's Food Writing and the Archive of Black Women's History," in Wallach, *Dethroning the Deceitful Pork Chop*, 33.

23. The Schomburg Center acquired S. Thomas Bivins's *The Southern Cook Book*, but likely after the bibliophile's death. Maira Liriano and I inspected the different bookplates on various cookbooks together, she noting that the varying designs afforded clues into the approximate date of acquisition. Steven Fullwood, associate curator of manuscripts at the Schomburg, also showed me various designs in the hopes that some of the few volumes I located would possess such identification—none did.

24. Forrest Parker, "The Lost Recipe of William Deas," *Undiscovered Charleston*, March 13, 2012, https://undiscoveredcharleston.com/2012/03/13/the-lost-recipe -of-william-deas/. The "lost recipe" Parker records is not for Charleston's vaunted "she-crab soup" but the shrimp soup listed on Schomburg's menu.

25. Michel Trouillot's reflections on the ability of what is available—and what is left uncollected—to shape history are now well known. As he observed, "silences enter the process of historical production at four crucial moments [most notably] the moment of fact assembly (the making of *archives*); the moment of fact *retrieval*

(the making of narratives)." Trouillot, "The Power in the Story," in *Silencing the Past: Power and the Production of History* (Boston: Beacon, 2015), 26. Schomburg was presented not only with actually silenced past cooks but also with archival aporia.

26. Everett Presson, personal communication, July 20, 2018.

27. Minnie C. Fox, ed., *The Blue Grass Cookbook* (New York: Duffield, 1904), v. Subsequent references will be given parenthetically within the text.

28. They are "Aunt Frances" (64) and "Aunt Maria" (120). The "Curing Hams" photograph is of a man preparing the pork (98); that said, the percentage of identified chefs by gender varies significantly (one of four women depicted is named, as compared to one of two men).

29. The unwillingness to credit Black women's culinary achievements in these early twentieth-century southern cookbooks as an instance of intragender competition seems reasonable considering the continued documented exposés by Idella Parker (of Marjorie Kinnan Rawlings) and Dora Charles (of Paula Deen). See, for example, Kim Severson, "Paula Deen's Cook Tells of Slights, Steeped in History," *New York Times*, July 24, 2013, http://www.nytimes.com/2013/07/25/us/paula-deens-soul -sister-portrays-an-unequal-bond.html?_r=0.

30. The copy of the *Blue Grass Cook Book* in the offsite storage of the New York Public Library has no marks indicating that it was ever owned by the library's Division of Negro Literature, History and Prints, although that can't be ruled out; a stamp on the back inside cover reads November 11, 1932, meaning the book was acquired during Schomburg's lifetime. Call #VTI 1904/scan 3 3433 05693120.

31. Schomburg refers to both a Dan Singleton (4) and Bill Singleton (5); whether they are related or whether Schomburg erroneously uses both given names for the same chef is unknown. Additional information on Chef Singleton has yet to be located, although a history of the "Stage Coach Inn" in which he worked is in progress. Thanks to Melay Araya, my research assistant.

32. See the *Oyster Bay Enterprise-Pilot* for July 21, 2006 (online edition), which ran an article on the history of the colonial-era home in which the Stage Coach Inn was located between 1924 and 1941. Originally located at http://www.antonnews.com /oysterbayenterprisepilot/2006/07/21/news/ (no longer available).

33. The books of scholars such as Jessica B. Harris, Doris Witt, Psyche Williams-Forson, and Frederick Douglass Opie, to name four key figures, have of course taken up Schomburg's challenge. Recently Katharine Vester argued for the acknowledgment of Freda DeKnight's cookbook *A Date with a Dish* (1948) as the earliest published such overview of diasporan cuisine, as DeKnight included recipes from Cuba "placing . . . African American cooking within a diasporic frame." Vester, "A Date with a Dish: Revisiting Freda DeKnight's African American Cuisine," in Wallach, *Dethroning the Deceitful Pork Chop*, 57.

34. Laura Helton recently discovered Schomburg catalogs in the Fisk University library, but their contents are not yet publicly available. Elinor Des Verney Sinnette

discusses Schomburg's decades of collecting the documents that would become the core of the present Schomburg Center of the New York Public Library. See Sinnette, *Arthur Alfonso Schomburg*, for a detailing of Schomburg's bibliophilia and fellow collectors, 73–102, and his boyhood vow to debunk the racism of a schoolteacher, 13–14. It is possible that these works remained in his home or personal collection. According to Sinnette, "a considerable number of [Arthur Schomburg's] personal papers were destroyed after his death when his Brooklyn home was rented" (3). As noted earlier, family members do not recall any such books or culinary interests.

35. Sinnette, *Arthur Alfonso Schomburg*, 58–61.

36. *The Negro Motorist's Green Guide*, an invaluable resource for Black Americans on the road from the late 1930s through the early 1960s, did not publish its first issue until 1936, making it unlikely but not impossible that Schomburg availed himself of its recommendations. For lodging and dining options in the years Schomburg traveled before the publication of the *Guide*, he would have had to rely on informal and Masonic networks and personal or business contacts. See the Schomburg's digitized collection: http://digitalcollections.nypl.org/collections/the-green-book#/?tab =about. For more on the guide as a travel resource in the pre–civil rights era, see the University of Michigan at Dearborn's website: http://www.autolife.umd.umich.edu /Race/R_Casestudy/Negro_motorist_green_bk.htm.

37. In the 1928 novel *Plum Bun*, Fauset's passing-for-white heroine stifles her resentment and anger when her wealthy WASP boyfriend demands that a Black family be denied seating at the East Village café where they are dining; New Yorker James Baldwin, in essays written in the 1950s, also refers to being denied service in area restaurants.

38. The famed Cotton Club did not serve African American patrons, a fact I first learned from my Harlem-dwelling grandmother. For reasons perhaps known by other foodways scholars, its menu offered "Chinese" and "American" dishes. For a menu from the club dated 1925, see http://menus.nypl.org/menus/30937. In his blog, Frederick Douglass Opie provides background on Tillie's Chicken Shack, the establishment to which Schomburg refers: http://www.fredopie.com/food/odasalens.com /2013/08/tillies-chicken-shack-of-harlem.html.

Bibliography

Abrahams, M. H., and Geoffrey Galt Harpham. *A Glossary of Literary Terms*, 8th ed. Boston: Wadsworth, 2005.

Adams, Carol J. *The Sexual Politics of Meat: A Feminist-Vegetarian Critical Theory*, 10th anniversary edition. New York: Continuum, 2000.

Allen, Will, with Charles Wilson. *The Good Food Revolution: Growing Healthy Food, People, and Communities*. New York: Gotham, 2012.

Andrews, William L. "Reunion in the Postbellum Slave Narrative: Frederick Douglass and Elizabeth Keckley." *Black American Literature Forum*, 23, no. 1 (Spring 1989): 85–86.

Armstead, Myra B. Young. *"Lord, Don't Take Me in August": African Americans in Newport and Saratoga Springs, 1870–1930*. Urbana: University of Illinois Press, 1999.

Baldwin, James. "Notes of a Native Son." In *James Baldwin: Collected Essays*. Edited by Toni Morrison. New York: Library of America, 1998, 63–84.

Barth, Fredrik. *Ethnic Groups and Boundaries: The Social Organization of Culture Difference*. Boston: Little, Brown, 1969.

Beavers, Herman. *Wrestling Angels into Song: The Fictions of Ernest J. Gaines and James Alan McPherson*. Philadelphia: University of Pennsylvania Press, 1995.

Belasco, Warren. *Appetite for Change: How the Counterculture Took On the Food Industry*. 1989. Reprinted, Ithaca, NY: Cornell University Press, 1993.

Bishop, Marion. "Speaking Sisters: Relief Society Cookbooks and Mormon Culture." In *Recipes for Reading: History, Stories, Community Cookbooks*. Edited by Anne L. Bower. Amherst: University of Massachusetts Press, 1997, 89–104.

Bivins, Thomas. *The Southern Cookbook: A Manual of Cooking and List of Menus, Including Recipes Used by Noted Colored Cooks and Prominent Caterers*. Hampton, VA: Press of the Hampton Institute, 1912.

Bourdieu, Pierre. *Distinction: A Social Critique of the Judgement of Taste*. Translated by Richard Nice. Cambridge, MA: Harvard University Press, 1984.

Bower, Anne L., ed. *African American Foodways: Explorations of History and Culture*. Champaign: University of Illinois Press, 2008.

———. *Recipes for Reading: Community Cookbooks, Stories, Histories*. Amherst: University of Massachusetts Press, 1997.

Bragg, Rick. "Atlanta Journal: A Delicacy of the Past Is a Winner at Drive-In." *New York Times*, November 10, 1996. https://www.nytimes.com/1996/11/10/us /a-delicacy-of-the-past-is-a-winner-at-drive-in.html.

Brown, Gillian. "Someone's in the Kitchen with Dinah: Domestic Politics in *Uncle Tom's Cabin*." *American Quarterly* 38 (1986): 668–74.

Bullock Jr., Thomas. *The Ideal Bartender*. Saint Louis: Buxton & Skinner, 1917.

Butler, Cleora. *Cleora's Kitchens and Eight Decades of Great American Food: The Memoir of a Cook*. Tulsa, OK: Council Oak Books, 1985.

Campbell, Thomas Monroe. *The Movable School Goes to the Negro Farmer*. 1936. Reprinted, New York: Arno Press/New York Times, 1969.

Campbell, Tunis Gulic. *Hotel Keepers, Head Waiters, and Housekeepers' Guide*. Boston: Coolidge & Wiley, 1848.

———. *Sufferings of the Rev. T. G. Campbell and His Family*. Georgia, WA: Enterprise, 1877.

Cardon, Lauren S. "From Black Nationalism to the Ethnic Revival: *Meridian's* Lynne Rabinowitz." *MELUS* 36, no. 30 (Fall 2001): 159–85.

Carney, Judith Ann. *Black Rice: The Origins of Rice Cultivation in the Americas*. Cambridge, MA: Harvard University Press, 2001.

Carney, Judith Ann, and Richard Nicholas Rosomoff. *In the Shadow of Slavery: Africa's Botanical Legacy in the Atlantic World*. Berkeley: University of California Press, 2010.

Carver, George Washington. "Autobiography," 1897, reel 1, George Washington Carver Papers at Tuskegee Institute, Tuskegee, Alabama.

———. *Bulletin #7. Cotton Growing on Sandy Uplands Soils*. Tuskegee, AL: Tuskegee University, 1905. http://archive.tuskegee.edu/archive/handle/123456789/200

———. *Bulletin #27. When, What, and How to Can and Preserve Fruits and Vegetables in the Home*. Tuskegee, AL: Tuskegee University, 1915. http://archive .tuskegee.edu/archive/bitstream/handle/123456789/235

———. *Bulletin #32. Three Delicious Meals Every Day for the Farmer*. Tuskegee, AL: Tuskegee University, 1916. http://archive.tuskegee.edu/archive/bitstream /handle/123456789/243

———. *Bulletin #33. Twelve Ways to Meet the New Economic Conditions in the South*. Tuskegee, AL: Tuskegee University, 1917. http://archive.tuskegee.edu /archive/bitstream/handle/123456789/244

———. *Bulletin #34. Forty-Three Ways to Save the Wild Plum Crop*. Tuskegee, AL: Tuskegee University, 1917. http://archive.tuskegee.edu/archive/ bitstream /handle/123456789/245

———. *Bulletin #36. How to Grow the Tomato and 115 Ways to Prepare It for the*

Table. Tuskegee, AL: Tuskegee University, 1918. http://archive.tuskegee.edu
/archive/bitstream/handle/123456789/243

———. *Bulletin #39. How to Make and Save Money on the Farm*. Tuskegee, AL:
Tuskegee University, 1927. http://archive.tuskegee.edu/archive/bitstream
/handle/123456789/258

———. *Bulletin #43. Nature's Garden for Victory and Peace*. Tuskegee, AL: Tuskegee
University, 1942. http://archive.tuskegee.edu/archive/bitstream
/handle/123456789/262

———. *The Canning and Preserving of Fruits and Vegetables in the Home*. Tuskegee,
AL: Tuskegee Normal and Industrial Institute, 1912.Cavitch, Max. *American
Elegy: The Poetry of Mourning from the Puritans to Whitman*. Minneapolis:
University of Minnesota Press, 2007.

de Certeau, Michel. *The Practice of Everyday Life*. Translated by Stephen Rendell.
Berkeley: University of California Press, 1984.

Chatelain, Marcia. "Black Women's Food Writing and the Archive of Black
Women's History." In *Dethroning the Deceitful Pork Chop: Rethinking African
American Foodways from Slavery to Obama*. Edited by Jennifer Jensen Wallach.
Fayetteville: University of Arkansas Press, 2015, 58–73.

Childs, John Brown. "Afro-American Intellectuals and the People's Culture."
Journal of Theory and Society 13 (1984): 69–90.

Clinton, Catherine. *The Plantation Mistress: Women's World in the Old South*. New
York: Pantheon, 1983.

Cooper, James Fenimore. *The Spy*. 1821. http://www.gutenberg.org/cache/epub
/9845/pg9845-images.html.

Counihan, Carole, ed. *Food in the U.S.A.: A Reader*. New York: Routledge, 2002.

Curtin, Deane W., and Lisa M. Heldke, eds. *Cooking, Eating, Thinking: Transformative Philosophies of Food*. Bloomington: Indiana University Press, 1992.

Darden, Carole, and Norma Jean Darden. *Spoonbread and Strawberry Wine*. New
York: Doubleday, 1978.

Deetz, Kelley Fanto. "Stolen Bodies, Edible Memories: The Influence and Function of West African Foodways in the Early British Atlantic." In *The Routledge
History of Food*. Edited by Carol Helstosky. New York: Routledge, 2015.

DeKnight, Freda. *A Date with a Dish: A Cook Book of American Negro Recipes*.
1948. Revised and reprinted as *The Ebony Cookbook: A Date with a Dish*.
Chicago: Johnson, 1962, 1973.

Dinius, Marcy J. "'Look!! Look!! At This!!!! The Radical Typography of David
Walker." *PMLA* 126, no. 1 (January 2011): 55–72.

Douglas, Mary. "Deciphering a Meal." *Daedalus* 101, no. 1 (Winter 1972): 61–81.

———. "Standard Social Uses of Food: Introduction." In *Food in the Social Order:
Studies of Food and Festivities in Three American Communities*. Edited by Mary
Douglas. New York: Russell Sage Foundation, 1984, 1–39.

Douglass, Frederick. *Narrative of the Life of Frederick Douglass, Written by Himself.*

1845. Reprinted in *Douglass: Autobiographies*. Edited by Henry Louis Gates Jr. New York: Library of America, 1994, 1–102.

Dunbar, Erika Armstrong. *Never Caught: The Washingtons' Relentless Pursuit of Their Runaway Slave, Ona Judge*. New York: Simon & Schuster, 2017.

Duncan, Russell. *Freedom's Shore: Tunis Campbell and the Georgia Freedmen*. Athens: University of Georgia Press, 1986.

Eble, Connie. "DARE and the Louisiana Purchase." *DARE [Dictionary of American Regional English] Newsletter* 6, no. 4 (Fall 2003): 1–4. http://dare.wisc.edu/sites/dare.wisc.edu/files/DARENEWS64.pdf.

Edge, John T. *The Potlikker Papers: A Food History of the Modern South*. New York: Penguin, 2017.

Egerton, Douglas R. *Death or Liberty: African Americans and Revolutionary America*. Oxford: Oxford University Press, 2009.

Egerton, John. *Southern Food: At Home, On the Road, In History*. 1987. Reprinted, with a new author's preface, Chapel Hill: University of North Carolina Press, 1993.

Fabre, Geneviève, and Robert O'Meally, eds. Introduction to *History and Memory in African-American Culture*. Oxford: Oxford University Press, 1994, 3–17.

Fauset, Jessie. *Plum Bun: A Novel without a Moral*. New York: Frederick Stokes, 1928.

Ferguson, Leland. *Uncommon Ground: Archaeology and Early African America, 1650–1800*. Washington, D.C.: Smithsonian Books, 1992.

Fisher, Abby. *What Mrs. Fisher Knows about Southern Cooking*. Reprinted with an introduction by Karen L. Hess. 1881. Bedford, MA: Applewood, 1995.

Foreman, Gabrielle P. "Manifest in Signs: The Politics of Sex and Representation in *Incidents in the Life of a Slave Girl.*" In *Harriet Jacobs and Incidents in the Life of a Slave Girl: New Critical Essays*. Edited by Deborah Garfield and Rafia Zafar. Cambridge: Cambridge University Press, 1996, 76–99.

Fox, Minnie C., ed. *The Blue Grass Cookbook*. New York: Duffield & Company, 1904.

Frantz, Rachel. *African American Business Leaders and Entrepreneurs*. New York: Facts on File, 2004, 51–53.

Frienz, D. J. [Dianna Seay]. *173 Pre-Prohibition Cocktails: Potations So Good They Scandalized a President*. Jenks, OK: Howling at the Moon Press, 2001.

Froula, Christine. "Mrs. Dalloway's Postwar Elegy: Women, War, and the Art of Mourning." *Modernism/modernity* 9, no. 1 (2002): 125–63.

Gaines, Ernest J. *A Gathering of Old Men*. 1983. Reprinted, New York: Vintage, 1984.

Gaskins, Ruth L. *A Good Heart and a Light Hand: Ruth L. Gaskins' Collection of Traditional Negro Recipes*. Annandale, VA: Turnpike, 1968.

Geertz, Clifford. "Thick Description: Toward an Interpretative Theory of Culture." In *The Interpretation of Cultures: Selected Essays*. New York: Basic Books, 1973.

Genovese, Eugene D. *Roll, Jordan, Roll: The World the Slaves Made*. 1974. Reprinted, New York: Vintage, 1976.

Gikandi, Simon. *Slavery and the Culture of Taste*. Princeton, NJ: Princeton University Press, 2011.

Glover, E. T. *The Warm Springs Receipt Book*. Richmond, VA: Johnson, 1897.

Goldman, Anne. "'I Yam What I Yam': Cooking, Culture, and Colonialism." In *De/Colonizing the Subject: The Politics of Gender in Women's Autobiography*. Edited by Sidonie Smith and Julia Watson. Minneapolis: University of Minnesota Press, 1992, 169–95.

———. *Take My Word: Autobiographical Innovations of Ethnic American Working Women*. Berkeley: University of California, 1996.

Gordon-Reed, Annette. *The Hemingses of Monticello: An American Family*. New York: Norton, 2008.

Hall, Franklin H. *How to Make and Serve 100 Choice Broths and Soups*. Philadelphia: Christian Banner Print, 1903.

———. *300 Ways to Cook and Serve Shellfish*. Philadelphia: Christian Banner Print, 1901.

Halloran, Vivian Nun. "Introduction: Novels as Museums in a Postmodern Age." In *Exhibiting Slavery: The Caribbean Postmodern Novel as Museum*. Charlottesville: University of Virginia Press, 2009, 1–20.

Halttunen, Karen. *Confidence Men and Painted Women: A Study of Middle-Class Culture in America, 1830–1870*. New Haven, CT: Yale University Press, 1982.

Harris, Jessica B. "Heirloom Recipes from a Southern Family: A Big-Flavored Meal in the African-American Tradition." *Food and Wine*, February 1991.

———. *High on the Hog: A Culinary Journey from Africa to America*. New York: Bloomsbury, 2011.

———. *Iron Pots and Wooden Spoons: Africa's Gifts to New World Cooking*. New York: Atheneum, 1989.

Haskins, Frederic. "Fraunces' Tavern." *Evening Star*, August 11, 1916.

Hern, Lafcadio. La cuisine creole: aa collection of culinary recipes from leading chefs and noted Creole housewives, who have made New Orleans famous for its cuisine. New Orleans: F. F. Hansell & Bro., Ltd, 1885.

Heldke, Lisa A. *Exotic Appetites: Ruminations of a Food Adventurer*. New York: Routledge, 2003.

———. "Foodmaking as a Thoughtful Practice." In *Cooking, Eating, Thinking: Transformative Philosophies of Food*. Edited by Deane W. Curtin and Lisa M. Heldke. Bloomington: Indiana University Press, 1992.

Hersey, Mark. *My Work Is That of Conservation: An Environmental Biography of George Washington Carver*. Athens: University of Georgia Press, 2011.

Hess, Karen L. *The Carolina Rice Kitchen: The African Connection*. Columbia: University of South Carolina Press, 1992.

Hine, Darlene Clark. "Rape and the Inner Lives of Southern Black Women: Thoughts on the Culture of Dissemblance." In *Southern Women: Histories and Identities*. Edited by Virginia Bernhard, Betty Brandon, Elizabeth Fox-Genovese, and Theda Perdue. Columbia: University of Missouri Press, 1992.

Hoffman, Gretchen L. "How Are Cookbooks Classified in Libraries? An Examination of LCSH and LCC." *North American Symposium on Knowledge Organization* 4, no. 1 (2013): 88–103. Retrieved from http://journals.lib.washington.edu/index.php/nasko/article/view/14650.

———. "What's the Difference between Soul Food and Southern Cooking? The Classification of Cookbooks in American Libraries." In *Dethroning the Deceitful Pork Chop: Rethinking African American Foodways from Slavery to Obama*. Edited by Jennifer Jensen Wallach. Fayetteville: University of Arkansas Press, 2015.

Hoffnung-Garskoff, Jesse. "The World of Arturo Alfonso Schomburg." In *The Afro-Latin@ Reader: History and Culture in the United States*. Edited by Miriam Jiménez Román and Juan Flores. Durham, NC: Duke University Press, 2010, 70–91.

Holt, Rackham. *George Washington Carver: An American Biography*. New York: Doubleday, Doran, 1943.

Horton, James Oliver, and Lois E. Horton. *Black Bostonians*. New York: Holmes & Meier, 1999.

———. *In Hope of Liberty*. Oxford: Oxford University Press, 1998.

Hughes, Langston. "I, Too." In *Selected Poems of Langston Hughes*. New York: Vintage, 1990, 275.

Inness, Sherrie A., ed. *Kitchen Culture in America: Popular Representations of Food, Gender, and Race*. Philadelphia: University of Pennsylvania Press, 2001.

Johnson, James Weldon. "O Black and Unknown Bards." In *The Book of American Negro Poetry*. Edited by James Weldon Johnson. 1922. Reprint, New York: Harvest/Harcourt Brace, 1969, 73–74.

Jones, Ita. *The Grubbag: An Underground Cookbook*. New York: Vintage, 1971.

Joyce, Donald Franklin. *Gatekeepers of Black Culture*. Westport, CT: Greenwood, 1983.

Kalčik, Susan. "Ethnic Foodways in America: Symbol and the Performance of Identity." In *Ethnic and Regional Foodways in the United States: The Performance of Group Identity*. Edited by Linda Keller Brown and Kay Mussell. Knoxville: University of Tennessee Press, 1984, 37–65.

Kaplan, Caren. "Resisting Autobiography: Out-Law Genres and Transnational Feminist Subjects." In *Women, Autobiography, Theory: A Reader*. Edited by

Sidonie Smith and Julia Watson. Madison: University of Wisconsin Press, 1998, 208–16.

Kelly, Traci. "If I Were a Voodoo Priestess: Women's Culinary Autobiographies." In *Kitchen Culture in America: Popular Representations of Food, Gender, and Race.* Edited by Sherrie A. Inness. Philadelphia: University of Pennsylvania Press, 2001, 251–71.

King, Doris, ed. *"Never Let People Be Kept Waiting": A Textbook on Hotel Management.* Raleigh, NC: King Reprints in Hospitality Management, 1973.

Kremer, Gary R. *George Washington Carver in His Own Words.* Columbia: University of Missouri Press, 1987.

Leonardi, Susan J. "Recipes for Reading: Summer Pasta, Lobster à la Riseholme, and Key Lime Pie." *PMLA* 104, no. 3 (May 1989): 340–47.

Lewis, Earl. *In Their Own Interests: Race, Class, and Power in Twentieth-Century Norfolk, Virginia.* Chapel Hill: University of North Carolina Press, 1991.

Lewis, Edna. *The Taste of Country Cooking.* New York: Knopf, 1976.

———, "What Is Southern?" *Grantmakers in the Arts Reader: Ideas and Information on Arts and Culture* 19, no. 3 (Fall 2008): 3–4. Originally published in *Gourmet Magazine,* January 2008.

Linzie, Anna. *The True Story of Alice B. Toklas: A Study of Three Autobiographies.* Iowa City: University of Iowa Press, 2006.

Longone, Janice Bluestein. "Early Black-Authored American Cookbooks." *Gastronomica* 1, no. 1 (Winter 2001): 96–99.

———. "Romanced by Cookbooks." *Gastronomica* 4, no. 2 (May 2004): 35–42.

———. "Introduction." *A Domestic Cook Book: Containing a Careful Selection of Useful Receipts for the Kitchen* by Malinda Russell. *1866.* Reprint, Ann Arbor, MI: William L. Clements Library, 2007.

Lyford, Carrie Alberta. *A Book of Recipes for the Cooking School.* Hampton, VA: Hampton Normal and Agricultural Institute, 1921.

Malcolm, Janet. *Two Lives: Gertrude and Alice.* New Haven, CT: Yale University Press, 2007.

Martin, Martha. *The Weed's Philosophy and Other Poems.* Montreal, 1913.

McMurray, Linda. *George Washington Carver: Scientist and Symbol.* Oxford: Oxford University Press, 1981.

Mennella, Julie A., Coren P. Jagnow, and Gary K. Beauchamp. "Prenatal and Postnatal Flavor Learning by Human Infants." *Pediatrics* 107, no. 6 (2001): E88.

Miller, Adrian. *The President's Kitchen Cabinet: The Story of the African Americans Who Have Fed Our First Families, from the Washingtons to the Obamas.* Chapel Hill: University of North Carolina Press, 2017.

Moody, Anne. *Coming of Age in Mississippi.* 1968. Reprinted, New York: Delta, 2004.

Morrison, Toni. *Playing in the Dark*. New York: Vintage, 1993.

National Council of Negro Women. *Historical Cookbook of the American Negro*. Washington, D.C.: Corporate Press, 1958.

New York Public Library, *The Legacy of Arthur A. Schomburg: A Celebration of the Past, a Vision for the Future*. New York: NYPL Schomburg Center for Research in Black Culture, 1986.

Opie, Frederick Douglass. *From Hog to Hominy: Soul Food from Africa to America*. New York: Columbia University Press, 2008.

Paige, Howard. *Aspects of Afro-American Cookery*. Southfield, MI: Aspects, 1987.

Palmié, Stephan. *Wizards and Scientists: Explorations in Afro-Cuban Modernity and Tradition*. Durham, NC: Duke University Press, 2002.

Patterson, Betty Benton. *Mammy Lou's Cookbook*. New York: Robert McBride, 1931.

Petry, Ann. *The Street*. 1946. Reprinted, New York: Mariner, 1998.

Piersen, William. *Black Yankees: The Development of an Afro-American Subculture in Eighteenth-Century New England*. Amherst: University of Massachusetts Press, 1988.

Pilgrim, Danya. "Transforming Public Space: Black Men and Philadelphia Eating Culture." Unpublished manuscript. May 2017.

Pinderhughes, John. *Family of the Spirit Cookbook: Recipes and Remembrances from African-American Kitchens*. New York: Simon & Schuster, 1990.

Poe, Tracy N. "The Origins of Soul Food in Black Urban Identity: Chicago, 1915–1947." *American Studies International* 42, no. 2 (February 1999): 4–33.

[Potter, Eliza]. *A Hair-Dresser's Experience in High Life*. 1859. Reprinted, New York: Oxford University Press, 1988.

Prettyman, Quandra. "Come Eat at My Table: Lives with Recipes." *Southern Quarterly* 30, no. 2–3 (Winter–Spring 1992): 131–40.

Ramazani, Jahan. *Poetry of Mourning: The Modern Elegy from Hardy to Heaney*. Chicago: University of Chicago Press, 1994.

Ramsay, Courtney. "Louisiana Foodways in Ernest Gaines's *A Lesson before Dying*." *Folklife in Louisiana. Louisiana's Living Traditions. Louisiana Folklore Miscellany*, 1995, reprinted at http://www.louisianafolklife.org/LT/Articles_Essays/main_misc_gaines_foodways.html.

Roach, Joseph. *Cities of the Dead: Circum-Atlantic Performance*. New York: Columbia University Press, 1996.

Roberts, Robert. *The House Servants Directory: or, A Monitor for Private Families Comprising Hints on the Arrangement and Performance of Servants' Work*. Edited by Graham Hodges. Armonk, NY: M. E. Sharpe, 1998.

Romines, Ann. "Growing Up with the Methodist Cookbooks." In *Recipes for Reading: History, Stories, Community Cookbooks*. Edited by Anne L. Bower. Amherst: University of Massachusetts Press, 1997, 75–88.

Rozin, Elizabeth, and Paul Rozin. "Some Surprisingly Unique Characteristics of Human Food Preferences." In *Food in Perspective: Proceedings of the Third International Conference on Ethnological Food Research, Cardiff, Wales.* Edited by Alexander Fenton and Trefor Owen. Edinburgh: John Donald Publishers, 1981, 243–52.

Russell, Malinda. *A Domestic Cook Book: Containing a Careful Selection of Useful Receipts for the Kitchen.* 1866. Edited by Janice Longone. Ann Arbor, MI: William L. Clements Library, 2007.

Saillant, John. "'Remarkably Emancipated from Bondage, Slavery, and Death': An African American Retelling of the Puritan Captivity Narrative, 1820." *Early American Literature* 29, no. 2 (1996): 122–40.

Schenck, Celeste M. "Feminism and Deconstruction: Re-Constructing the Elegy." *Tulsa Studies in Women's Literature* 5, no. 1 (1986): 13–27.

Schmidt, Paul. "'As If a Cookbook Had Anything to Do with Writing'—Alice B. Toklas." *Prose* 8 (1974): 179–203.

Schomburg, Arthur Alfonso. "[Cookbook.]" Arthur A. Schomburg Papers. Box 12—Folder 2—Cook Book. 12 pages. Schomburg Center for Research in Black Culture, New York Public Library.

———. Letters by Arthur Schomburg 1914–1938. Arthur Alfonso Schomburg papers, Schomburg Center for Research in Black Culture, New York Public Library.

———. "The Negro Digs Up His Past." In *The New Negro.* Edited by Alain Locke. 1925. Reprinted, New York: Atheneum, 1970, 231–37.

———. "Our Pioneers." *New York Amsterdam News,* August 1, 1936.

Scott, Natalie. *Mirations and Miracles of Mandy: Some Favorite Louisiana Recipes.* New Orleans: Robert True, 1929.

Shange, Ntozake. *If I Can Cook / You Know God Can.* Boston: Beacon, 1998.

Sharpless, Rebecca. *Cooking in Other Women's Kitchens: Domestic Workers in the South, 1865–1960.* Chapel Hill: University of North Carolina Press, 2010.

Simon, Linda. *The Biography of Alice B. Toklas.* Garden City, NJ: Doubleday, 1977.

Sinnette, Elinor Des Verney. *Arthur Alfonso Schomburg: Black Bibliophile and Collector.* Detroit: New York Public Library/Wayne State University Press, 1989.

Smart-Grosvenor, Vertamae. *Black Atlantic Cooking.* Upper Saddle River, NJ: Prentice Hall, 1990.

———. *Vibration Cooking.* 1970. Revised and reprinted, New York: Ballantine, 1986, 1991.

Smith, Doris. "In Search of Our Mothers' Cookbooks: Gathering African-American Culinary Traditions." *Iris,* Fall/Winter 1991, 22–27. See also Witt, Doris.

Stein, Gertrude. *The Autobiography of Alice B. Toklas.* 1933. In *Stein: Writings, 1903–1932.* Edited by Catherine Stimpson and Harriet Chessman. New York: Library of America, 1998, 655–913.

Stepto, Robert B. *From Behind the Veil. A Study of Afro-American Narrative.*
    Urbana: University of Illinois Press, 1970.
Stowe, Harriet Beecher. *Uncle Tom's Cabin.* 1852. Reprinted, New York: Harper
    Classics, 1965.
Strasser, Susan. *Never Done. A History of American Housework.* With a new preface
    by the author. New York: Macmillan, 2013.
Stuckey, Sterling. *Slave Culture: Nationalist Theory and the Foundations of Black
    America.* Oxford: Oxford University Press, 1987.
Sutton, David. *Remembrance of Repasts: An Anthropology of Food and Memory.*
    London: Berg, 2001.
Temple, Christel. "The Emergence of Sankofa Practice in the United States: A
    Modern History." *Journal of Black Studies* 41, no. 1 (2010): 127–50.
Terry, Bryant. *Vegan Soul Food Kitchen: Fresh, Healthy, and Creative African
    American Cuisine.* Cambridge, MA: Da Capo, 2009.
Theophano, Janet. *Eat My Words: Reading Women's Lives through the Cookbooks
    They Wrote.* New York: Palgrave, 2002.
Tipton-Martin, Toni. "Introduction." *The Blue Grass Cook Book.* Minnie C. Fox
    with introduction by John Fox, Jr. Lexington: university Press of Kentucky,
    2014.
———. *The Jemima Code: Two Centuries of African American Cookbooks..* Austin:
    University of Texas Press, 2015.
Tocqueville, Alexis de. "Some Reflections on American Manners." In *Democracy in
    America* (1831). http://xroads.virginia.edu/~hyper/detoc/toc_indx.html.
Toklas, Alice B. *The Alice B. Toklas Cookbook.* 1954. Reprinted, New York: Harper
    Perennial, 1984.
———. *Staying on Alone: Letters of Alice B. Toklas.* Edited by Edward Burns. New
    York: Liveright, 1973.
———. *What Is Remembered.* New York: Holt, 1963.
Tompkins, Kyla Wazana. *Racial Indigestion: Eating Bodies in the Nineteenth
    Century.* New York: New York University Press, 2011.
Trollope, Frances. *Domestic Manners of the Americans* (1832). xroads.virginia.edu
    /~hyper/DETOC/FEM/trollope.htm.
Trouillot, Michel-Rolph. "The Power in the Story." In *Silencing the Past: Power and
    the Production of History.* Boston: Beacon, 2015. 1–30.
Truong, Monique. *The Book of Salt.* Boston: Houghton Mifflin, 2003.
Turner, Bertha, ed. *The Federation Cookbook: A Collection of Tested Recipes,
    Contributed by the Colored Women of the State of California.* Pasadena, 1910.
Turner, Patricia. *Ceramic Uncles and Celluloid Mammies: Black Images and Their
    Influence on Culture.* Berkeley: University of California Press, 1995.
Twitty, Michael. *The Cooking Gene: A Journey through African American Culinary
    History in the Old South.* New York: Amistad, 2017.

Tye, Diane. *Baking as Biography*. Montreal: McGill–Queen's University Press, 2010.

Valdés, Vanessa K. *Diasporic Blackness: The Life and Times of Arturo Alfonso Schomburg*. Albany: State University of New York Press, 2017.

Vester, Katharine. "A Date with a Dish: Revisiting Freda DeKnight's African American Cuisine." In *Dethroning the Deceitful Pork Chop: Rethinking African American Foodways from Slavery to Obama*. Edited by Jennifer Jensen Wallach. Fayetteville: University of Arkansas Press, 2015, 47–60.

Walker, Alice. *In Search of Our Mothers' Gardens: Womanist Prose*. New York: Harvest/HBJ, 1984.

———. *Meridian*. 1976. Reprinted, New York: Harvest, 2003.

Wallach, Jennifer Jensen. "Dethroning the Deceitful Pork Chop: Food Reform at Tuskegee Institute." In *Dethroning the Deceitful Pork Chop: Rethinking African American Foodways*. Edited by Jennifer Jensen Wallach. Fayetteville: University of Arkansas Press, 2015, 165–79.

Wallach, Jennifer Jensen, editor. *Dethroning the Deceitful Pork Chop: Rethinking African American Foodways*. Fayetteville, University of Arkansas Press, 2015.

Washington, Booker T. *Up from Slavery*. 1901. http://www.gutenberg.org/ebooks /2376.

Weiner, Mark. "Consumer Culture and Participatory Democracy: The Story of Coca-Cola during World War II." In *Food in the U.S.A. A Reader*. Edited by Carole Counihan. New York: Routledge, 2002, 123–41.

White, Shane. "'It Was a Proud Day': African-Americans, Festivals, and Parades in the North, 1741–1834." *Journal of American History* 81, no. 1 (June 1994): 13–50.

———. *Somewhat More Independent: The End of Slavery in New York City, 1770–1810*. Athens: University of Georgia Press, 1991.

Williams-Forson, Psyche A. *Building Houses Out of Chicken Legs: Black Women, Food, and Power*. Chapel Hill: University of North Carolina Press, 2006.

Wilson, Harriet. *Our Nig, or, Sketches from the Life of a Free Black*. Edited by P. Gabrielle Foreman and Reginald H. Pitts. 1859. Reprinted, London: Penguin Books, 2005.

Witt, Doris. *Black Hunger: Food and the Politics of U.S. Identity*. Oxford: Oxford University Press, 1999.

Woodard, Vincent. *The Delectable Negro: Human Consumption and Homoeroticism within U.S. Slave Culture*. Edited by Justin A. Joyce and Dwight A. McBride. New York: New York University Press, 2014.

Yaeger, Patricia. "Edible Labor." *Southern Quarterly* 30, no. 2–3 (Winter–Spring 1992): 150–59.

Zafar, Rafia. "Carver's Food Movement: How the Famous Botanist Paved the Way for Today's 'Sustainable Agriculture.'" *Common Reader*, May 8, 2015, https:// commonreader.wustl.edu/c/carvers-food-movement/.

———. "Elegy and Remembrance in the Cookbooks of Alice B. Toklas and Edna Lewis." *MELUS* 38, no. 4 (Winter 2013): 32–35.

———. "The Proof of the Pudding: Of Haggis, Hasty Pudding, and Transatlantic Influence." *Early American Literature* 31 (1996): 133–49.

———. "Recipes for Respect: Black Hospitality Entrepreneurs before World War I." In *African American Foodways*. Edited by Anne L. Bower. Urbana: University of Illinois Press, 2007, 139–52.

———. "The Signifying Dish." *Feminist Studies* 25, no. 2 (Summer 1999): 449–69.

———. "The Signifying Dish." In *Voix Ethniques/Ethnic Voices*, vol. 2. Le Concours du Conseil Scientifique de l'Université de Tours. *Groupe des Recherches Anglo-Américaines de Tours* 14 (1996): 73–84.

———. "What Mrs. Fisher Knows about Old Southern Cooking." *Gastronomica* 1, no. 4 (Fall 2001): 88–90.

———. "Verta Mae Reverses the Middle Passage." Unpublished paper. Delivered at the Modern Language Association meeting, December 1999.

———. *We Wear the Mask: African Americans Write American Literature, 1760–1870.* New York: Columbia University Press, 1997.

Zimmerman, Andrew. *Alabama in Africa: Booker T. Washington, the German Empire, and the Globalization of the New South.* Princeton, NJ: Princeton University Press, 2010.

Index

CPSIA information can be obtained
at www.ICGtesting.com
Printed in the USA
LVHW031619220219
608477LV00003B/339/P